GREAT BLUE HERONS

Studies for Wildlife Artists

Photography and Text

by

Al Lodwick

ISBN 9781514213490

DEDICATION

To Ann Lodwick, my wife and best friend for nearly thirty-eight years.

ACKNOWLEDGEMENTS

Scott Mies for encouragement and editorial advice.

Rachel Lodwick for the Mieswick, LLC logo.

Victoria Tubbs for the author's photograph.

INTRODUCTION

This book is the result of five years of nature photography in the biologically diverse central highlands of Arizona around Prescott. The Arizona highlands are not what most people imagine when they first think of Arizona. At the lowest level you find desert grassland. This gives way to Oak-Pinyon-Juniper woodland. Higher still are the tall Ponderosa Pines – a stand of trees stretching hundreds of miles in Arizona and New Mexico. At the highest levels you find Douglas Fir forest. Throughout the highlands you find an intermingling of both flora and fauna from both hotter and colder climates. For example, you can find hedgehog cacti growing at the roots of Ponderosa Pines.

Perched in the Ponderosa Pines and foraging along the edges of reservoirs you will find the Great Blue Heron. Though not abundant, they are commonly seen by even those taking causal walks or jogging.

The emphasis of this book is to depict scenes for wildlife artists that are not easily seen with the unaided eye. Examples of this are the position of the feet when taking off from water, how the eye moves outward when changing from a defensive to a foraging situation, and how the feathers of the wings and tail overlap.

The author hopes that non-artists will also enjoy the pictures and learn more about these magnificent birds and the habitats of the highlands of central Arizona.

Al Lodwick
Prescott, Arizona
June 2015

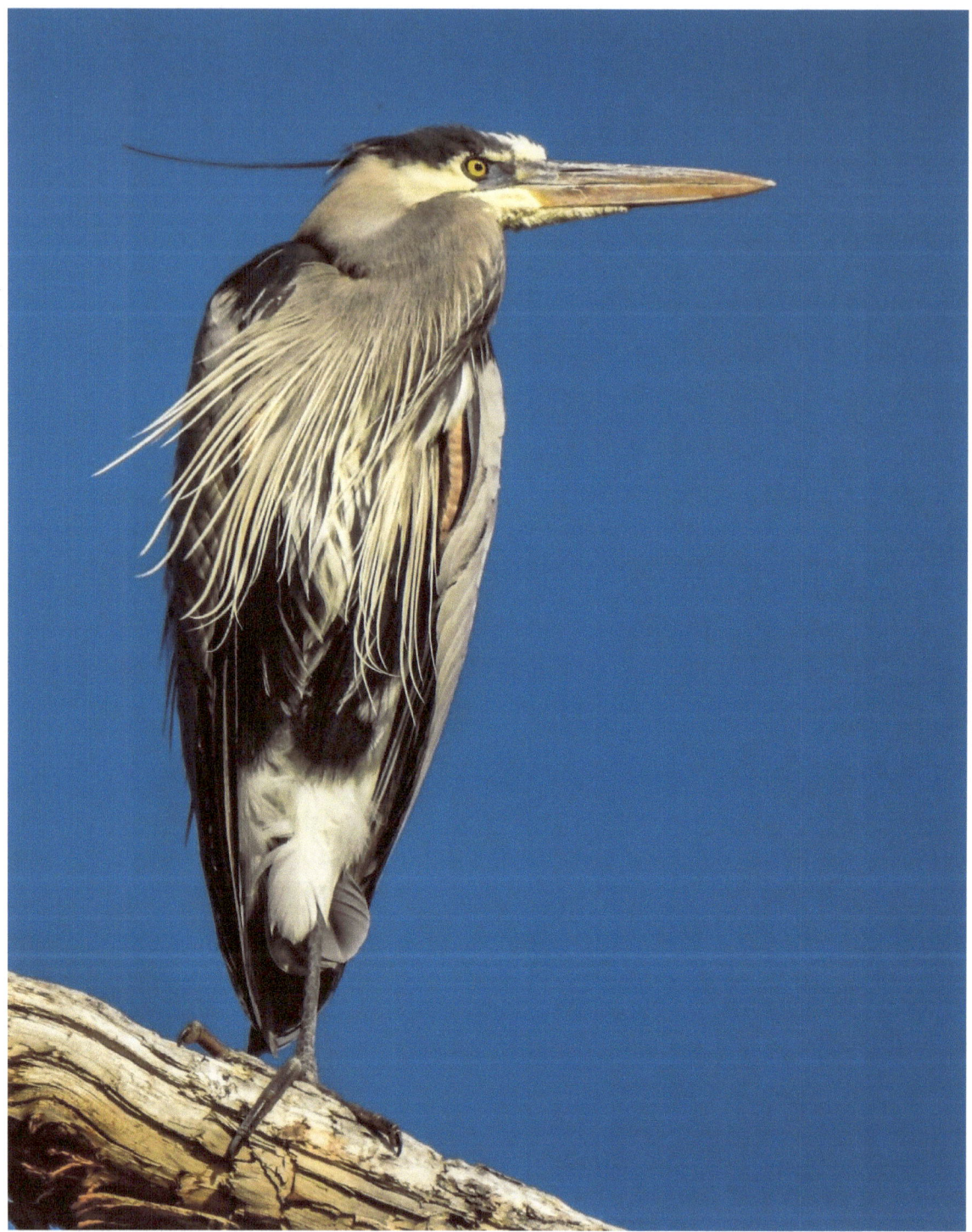

      Great Blue Herons are the largest herons in North America. They can grow to more than four feet tall and weigh up to about five pounds. They are not usually thought of as birds that perch in trees. However, as you will see in this book they are frequently found there. It is common for them to perch in this one-legged posture. This is an adult in breeding plumage.

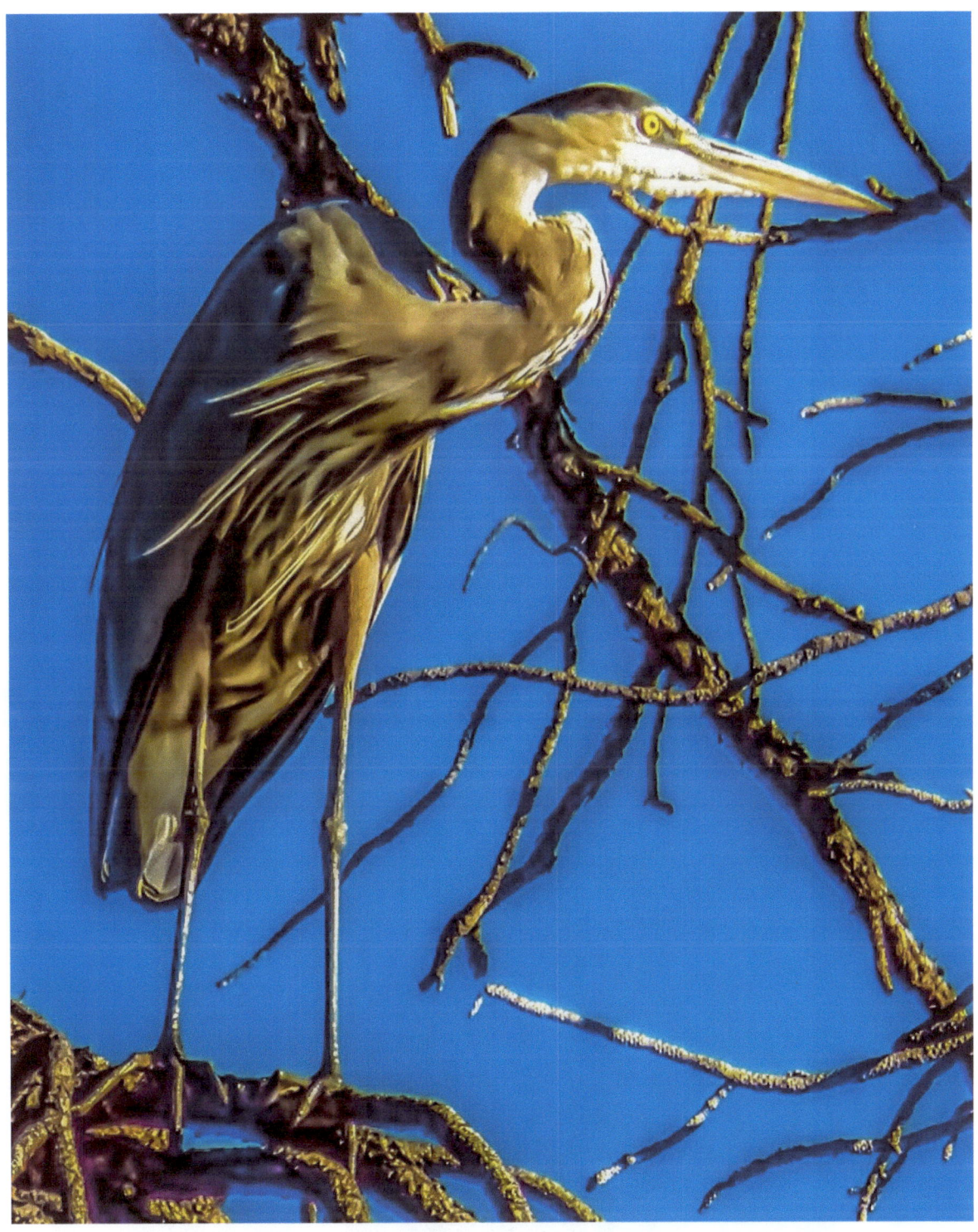

In this picture the bird is facing into a stiff breeze. Note that the feathers around the neck are blurred with the longer plumes being blown toward the back.

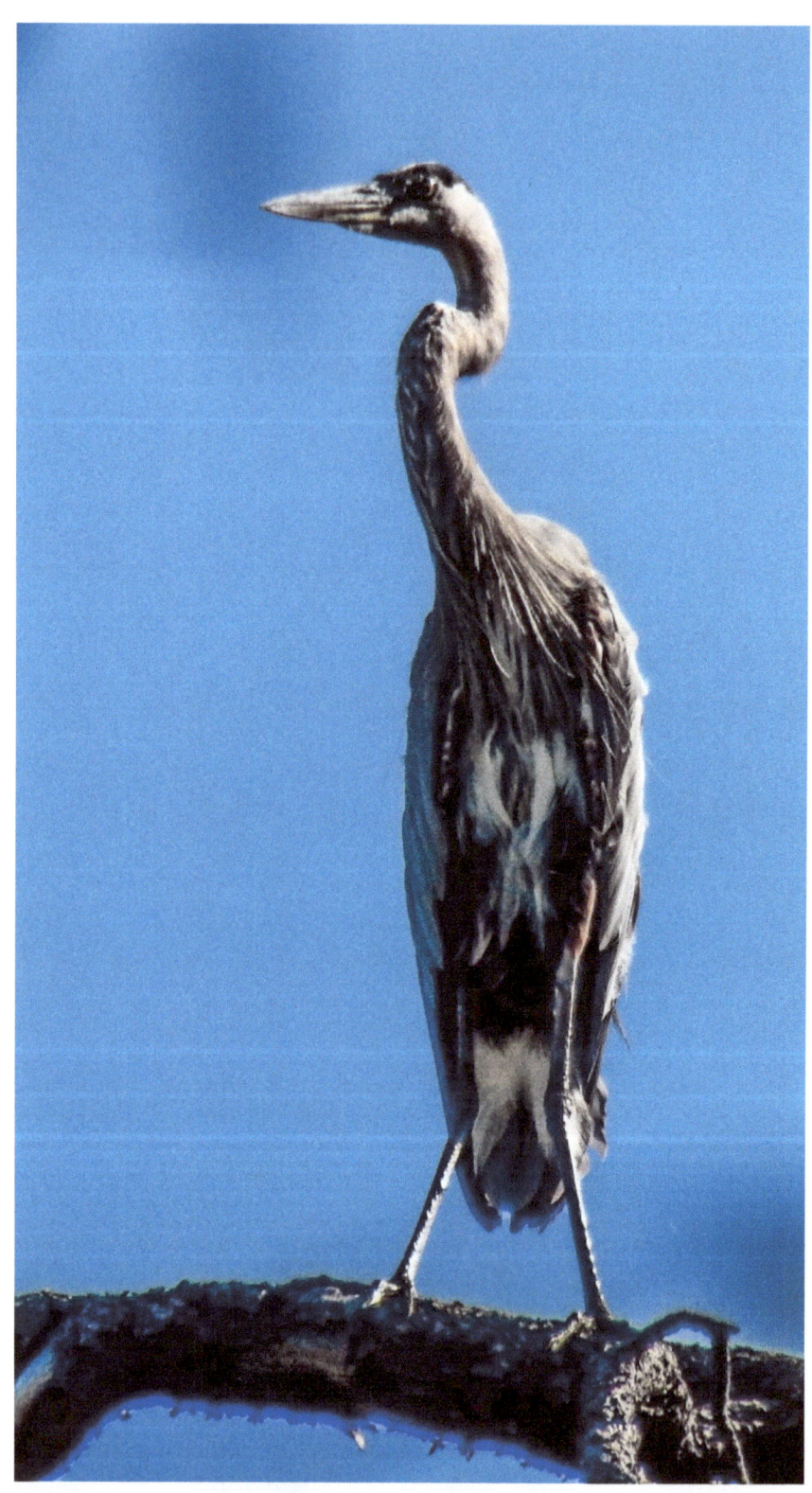

This is an immature bird. Note its shorter bill relative to the previous two pictures. It is molting from its fuzzy baby feathers to its first-year plumage.

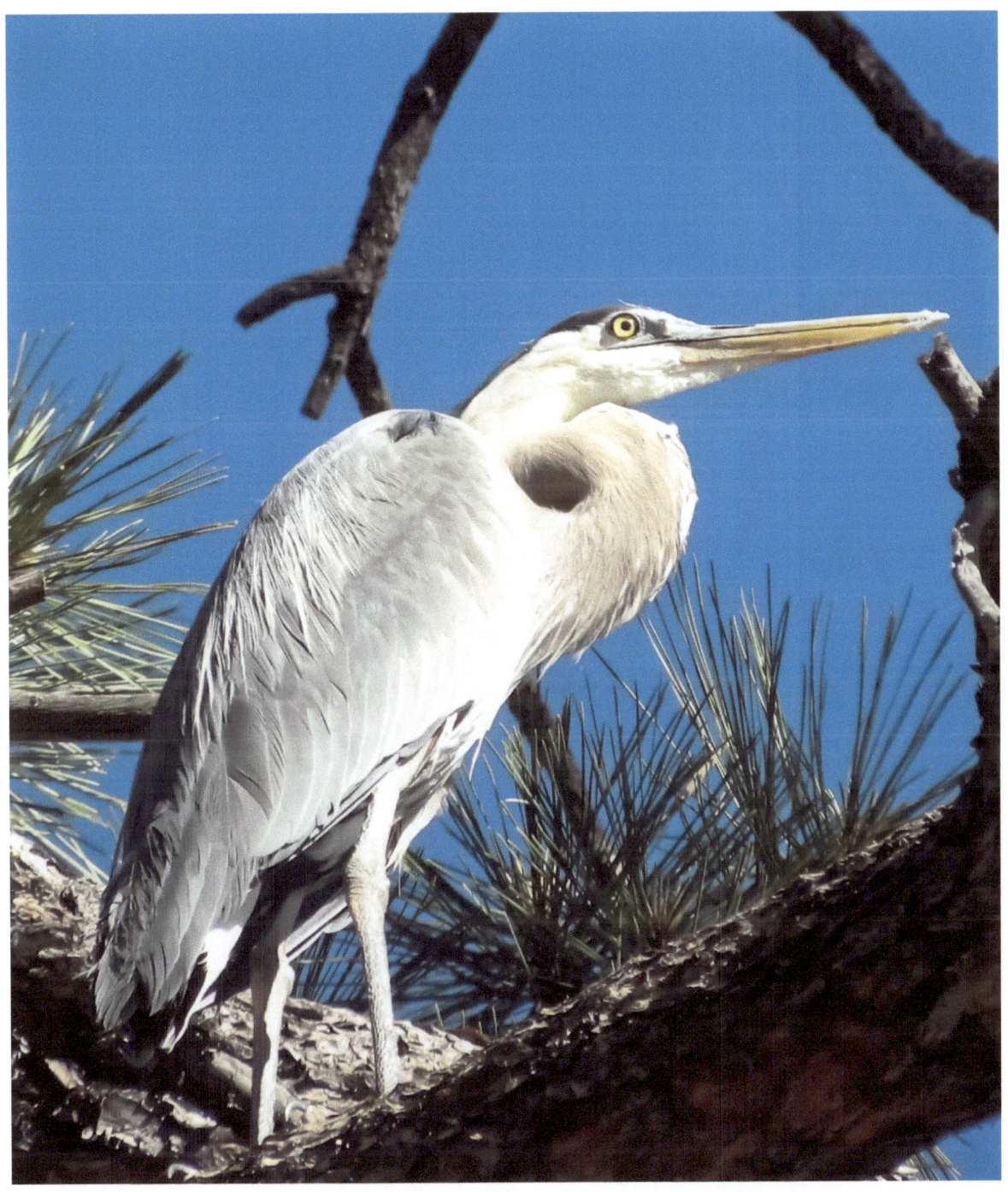

This Great Blue Heron is perched in a Ponderosa Pine tree. This is a scene typical of the highlands of central Arizona. They can be pictured in other trees appropriate to the area that you wish to depict. These birds are found throughout the United States and into southern Canada as well as Mexico.

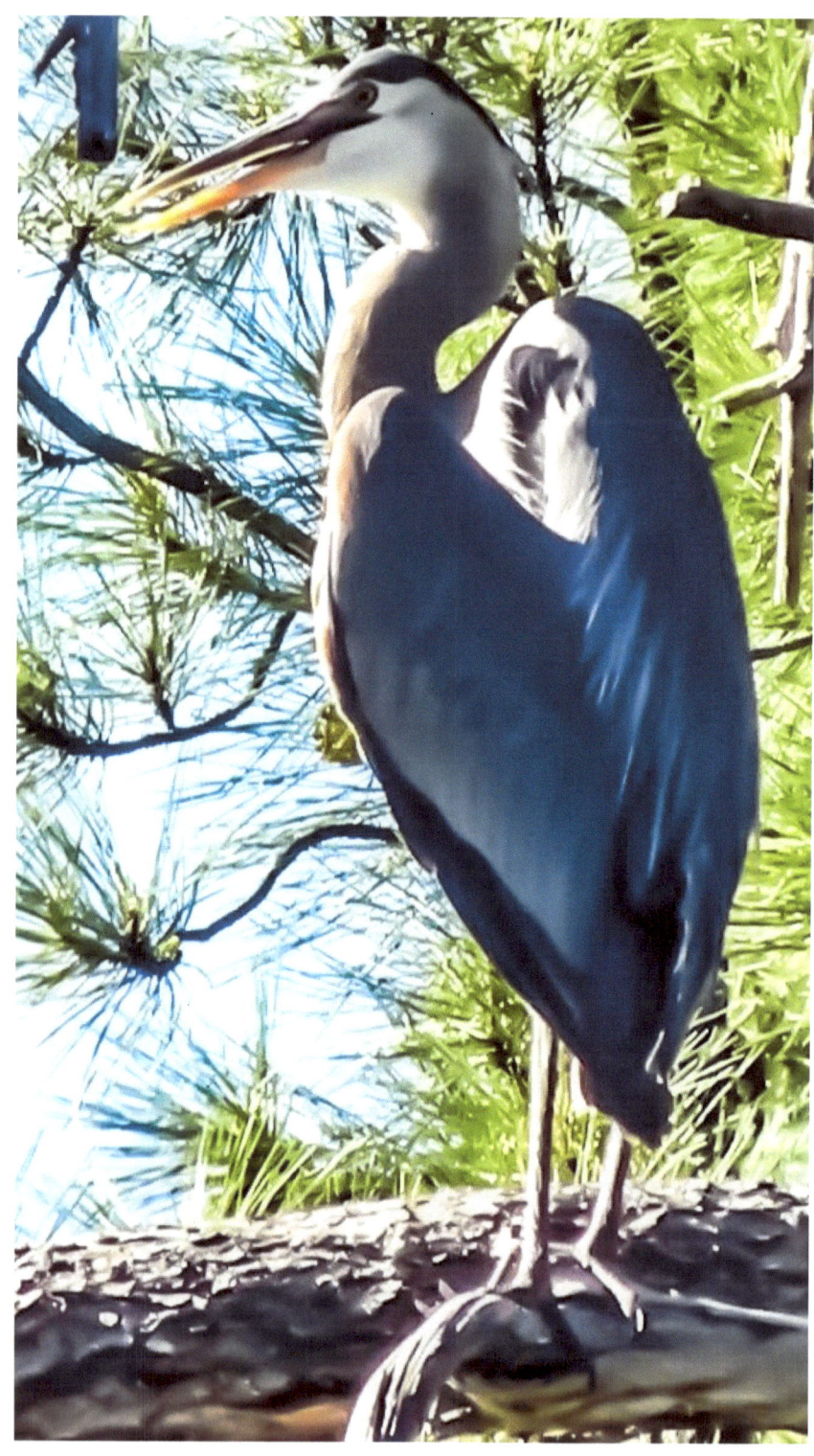

Something is irritating this bird. They usually only vocalize when they are startled or are in the nesting area. Note the tongue position when calling. The slightly raised wings indicate that it may be willing to make a stand but flight is also a possibility should the threat continue.

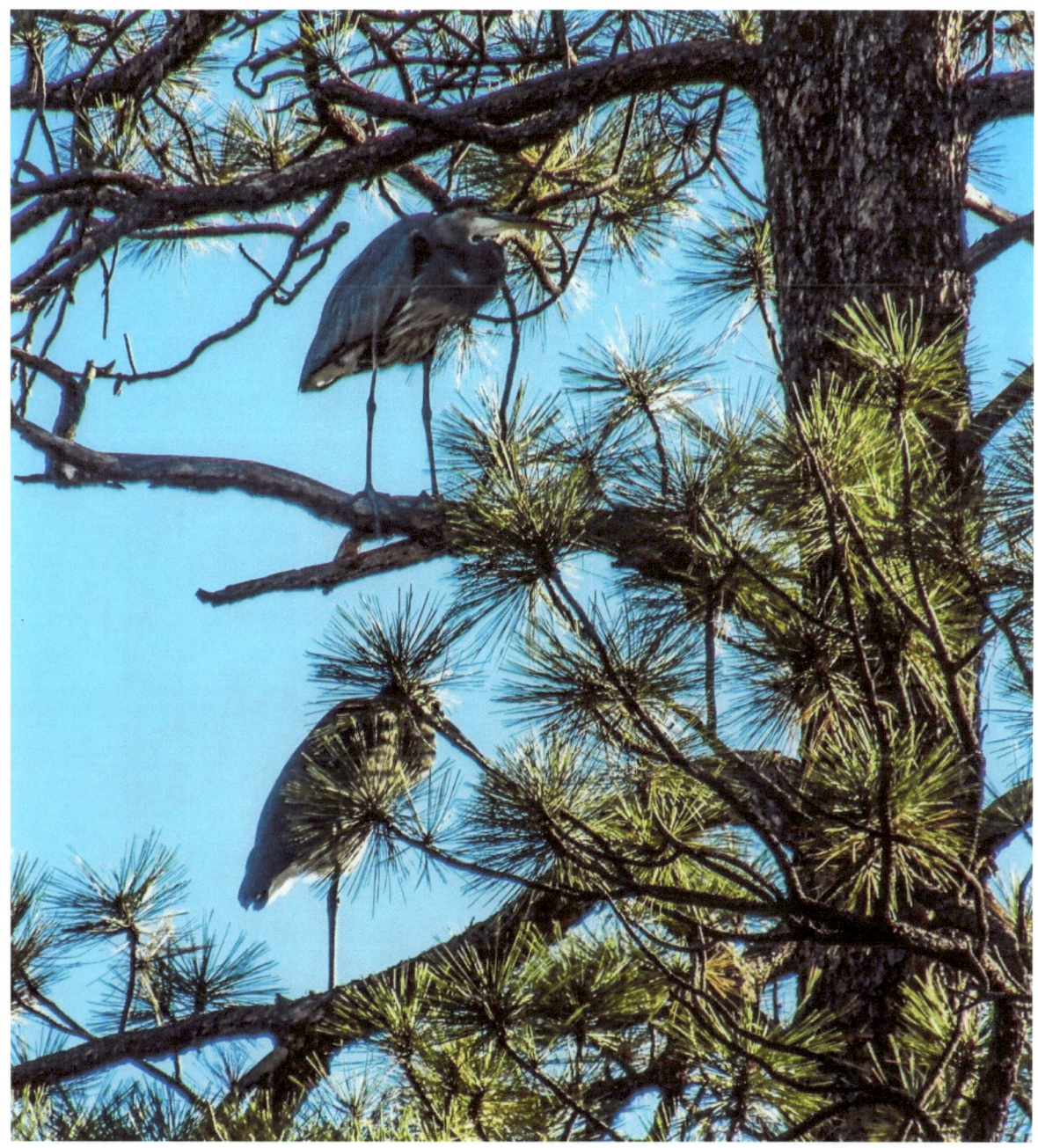

      Great Blue Herons are generally solitary birds but occasionally you will see them in pairs especially during the breeding season. Males and females are not easily distinguished in the field. These are perched in a Ponderosa Pine tree.

HEAD PROFILES

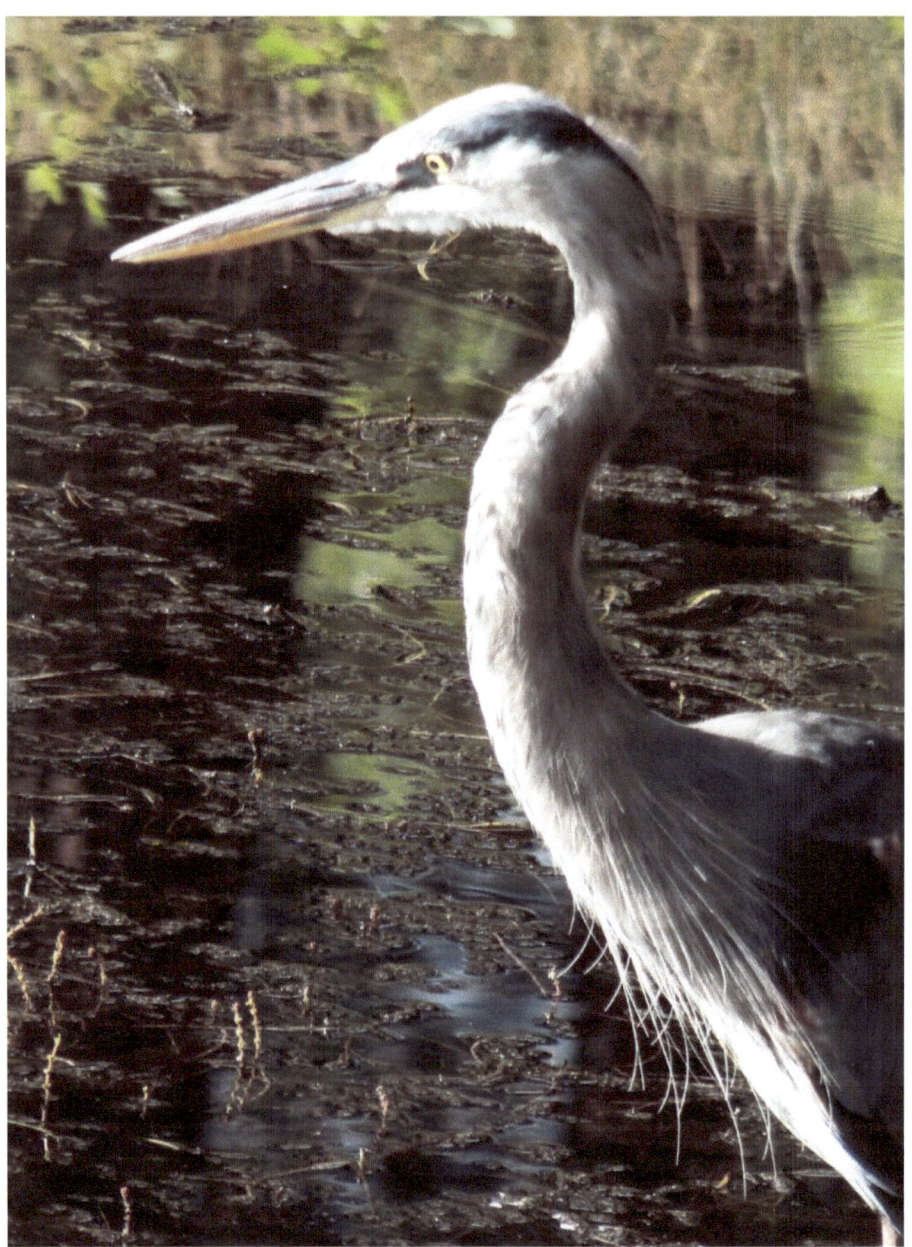

    This picture clearly shows how a Great Blue Heron is able to rotate its eyes to gain depth perception when it is foraging. The muscles behind the rear portion of the eye are able to push the back of the eyeball outward. Three dimensional vision is necessary to catch fast moving prey such as fish and frogs.

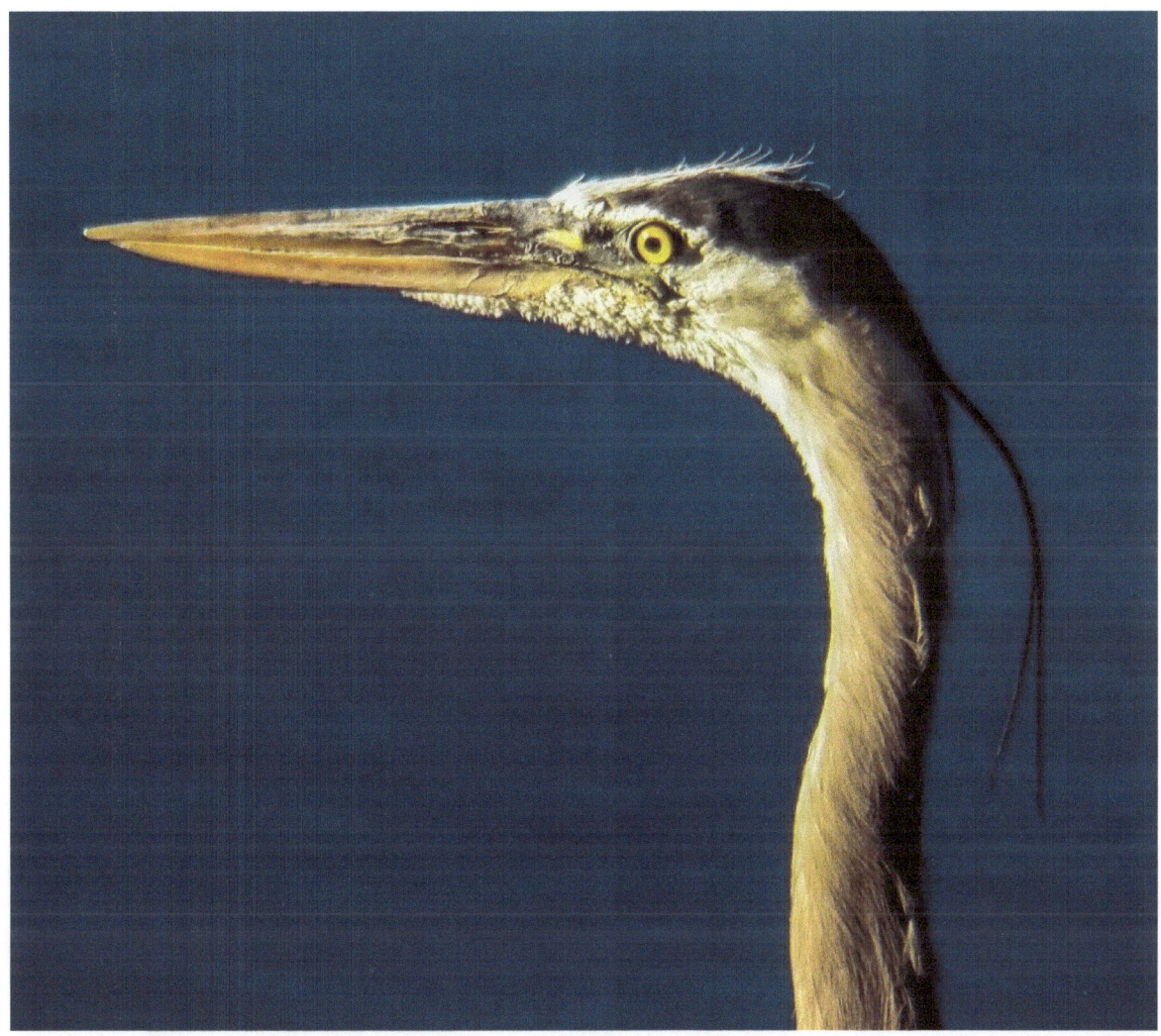

In this picture the bird seems to be looking more at the viewer than for prey. This is more of a defensive position than the previous picture. When danger is approaching three-dimensional vision is not important. All the bird needs to know is that danger is approaching and it needs to leave immediately. The rough looking feathers on the throat are the result of molting.

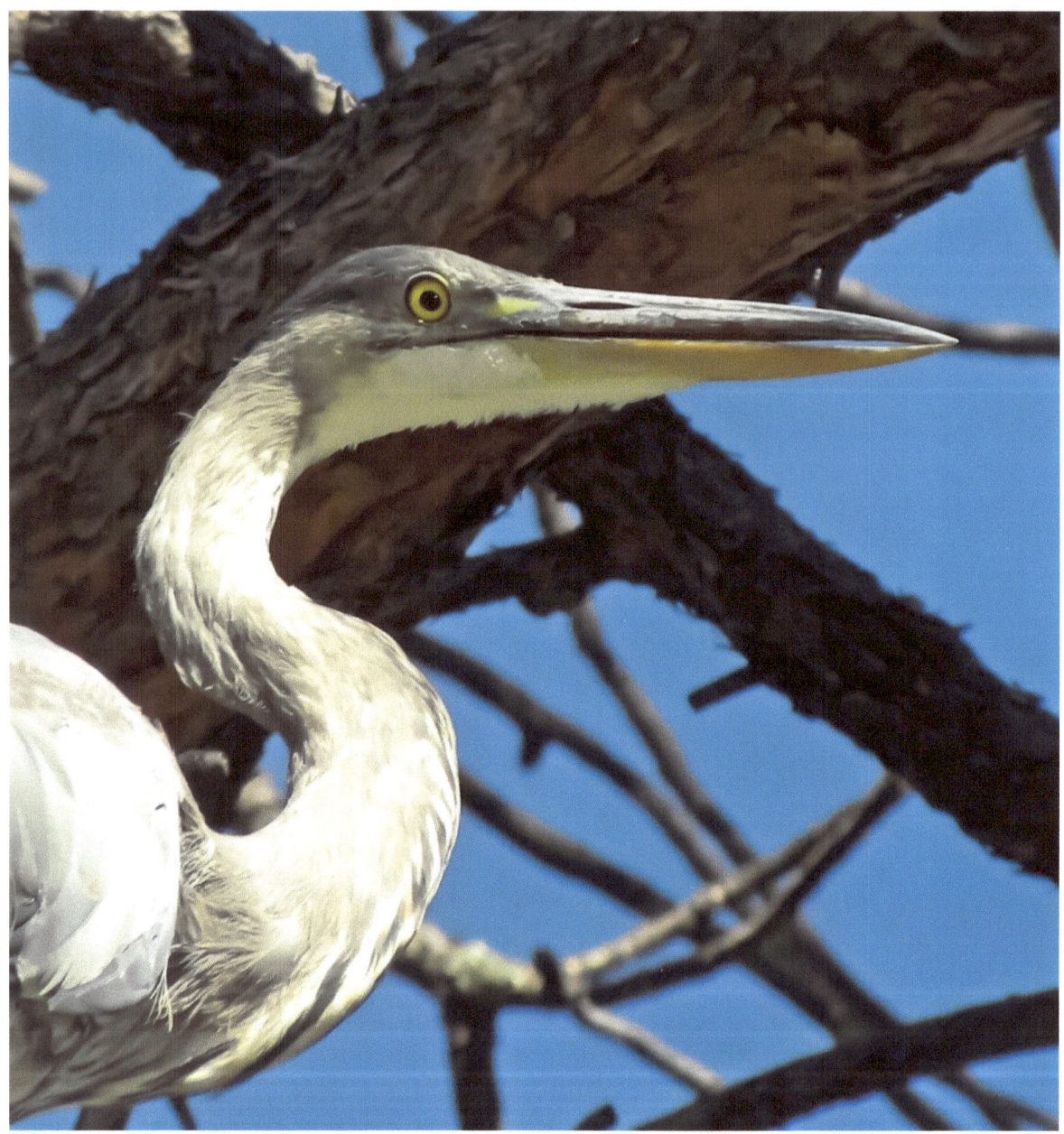

Here again we can see the eye looking directly at the viewer. Another advantage that the adaptation of movable eyes gives the Great Blue Heron is that it allows the bird to stand perfectly still when foraging. If it only needs to move it eyes, it is much less likely to be detected by its prey than if it had to swing its head back and forth.

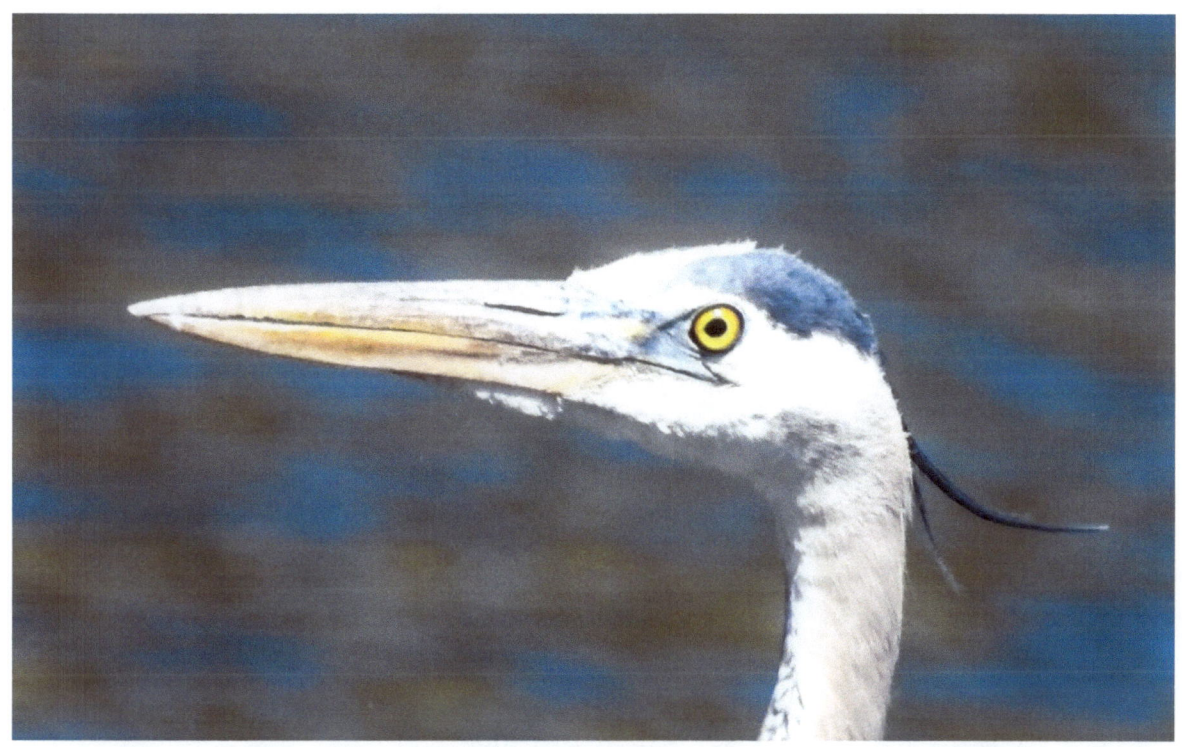

This picture was taken with an older camera so it is not quite the quality of the others. However, it does show how the long, trailing plume comes from the back of the back of the crown of the head. These plumes are more pronounced during the breeding season.

FORAGING

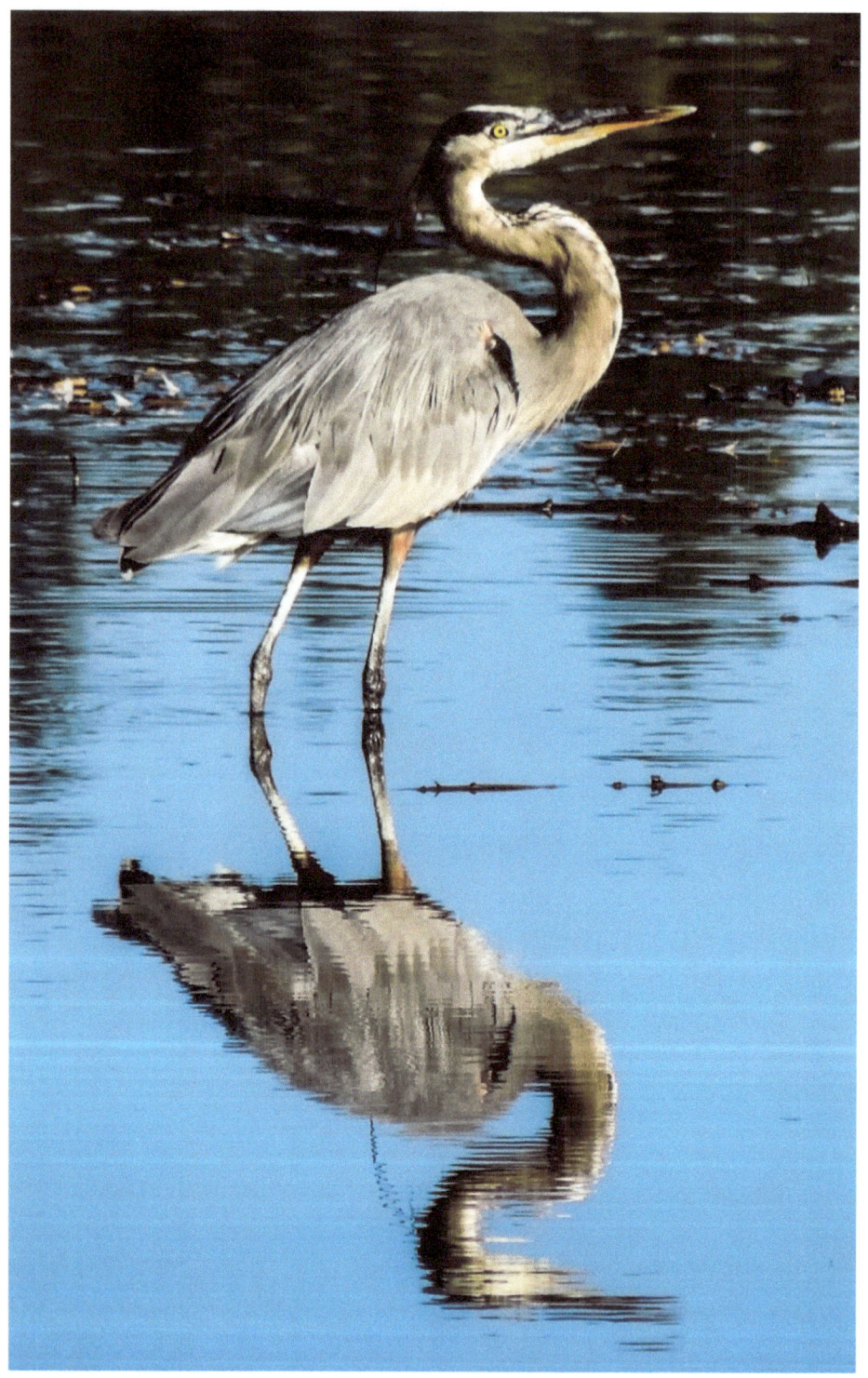

The primary ingredient in the diet of a Great Blue Heron is fish. However, given the opportunity for an easy catch, they will eat crayfish, insects, rodents, amphibians, reptiles, small birds and small mammals.

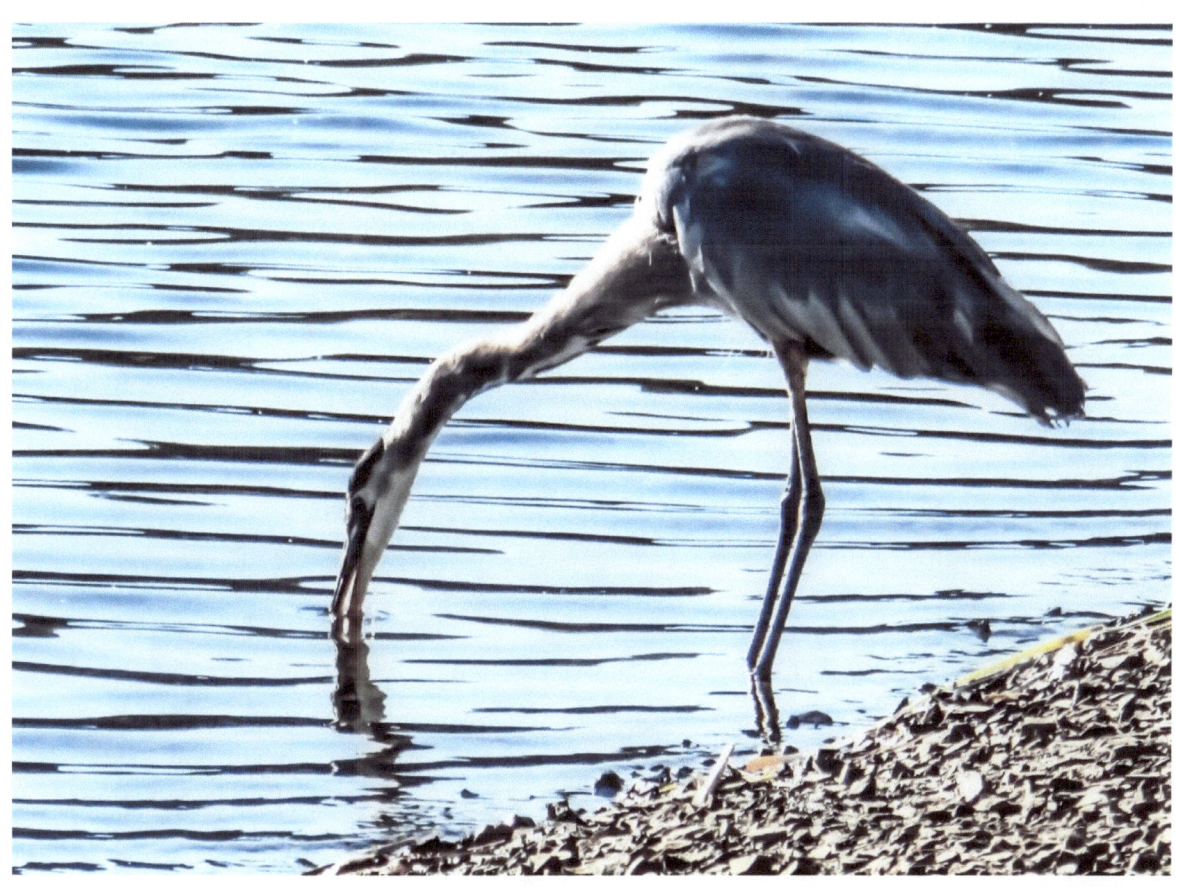

Great Blue Herons employ almost any means that you can think of for capturing prey. Here the bird appears to be pecking at the water in an attempt to cause a fish or insect to move from its hiding place. Its keen eyesight in three dimensions is the primary method of locating prey. They can even forage at night.

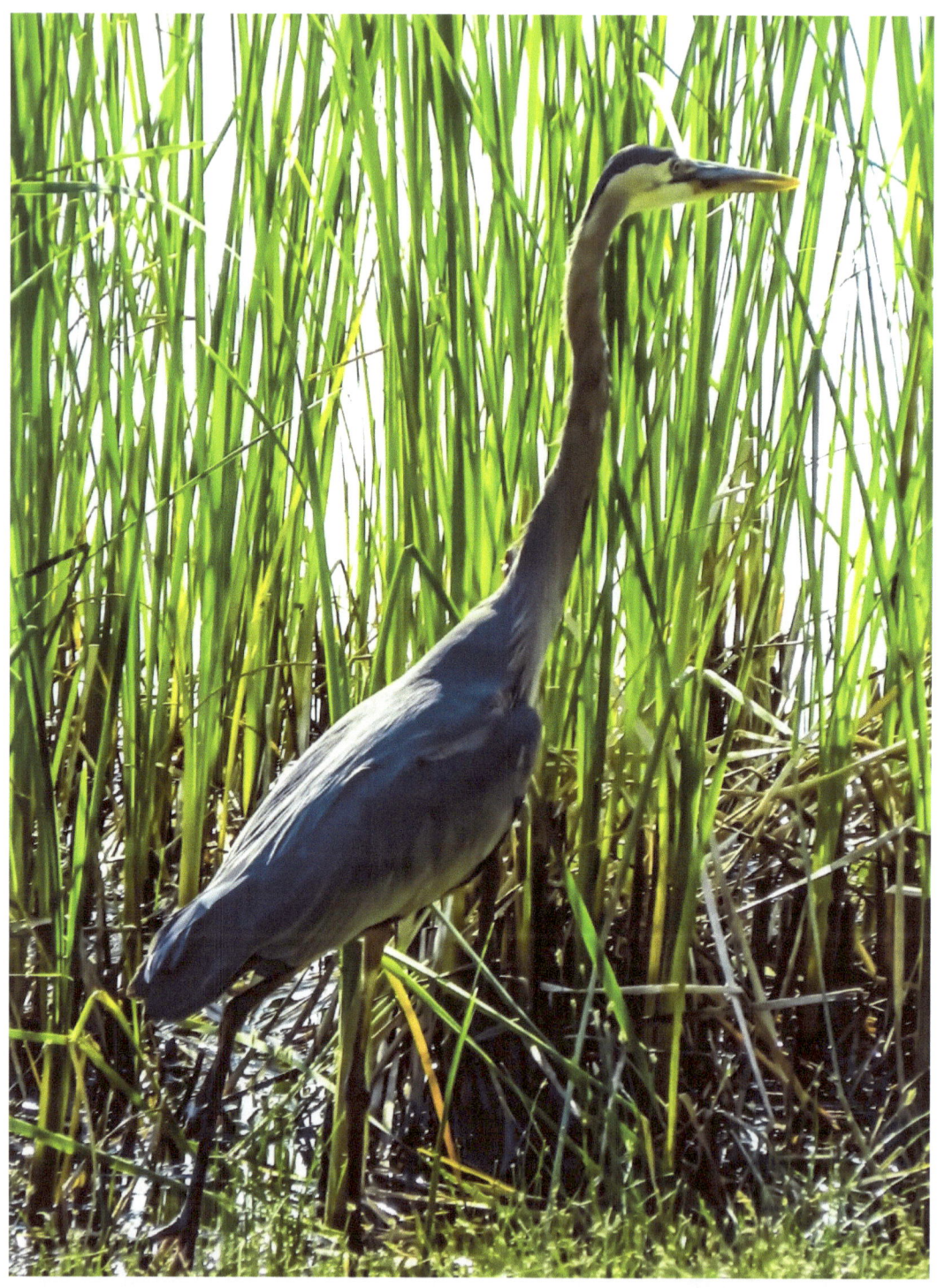

Cattails offer excellent cover for a foraging Great Blue Heron. Fish, amphibians and insects inhabit this environment. A bird may stand almost perfectly still for 15 to 30 minutes while waiting for suitable prey to approach.

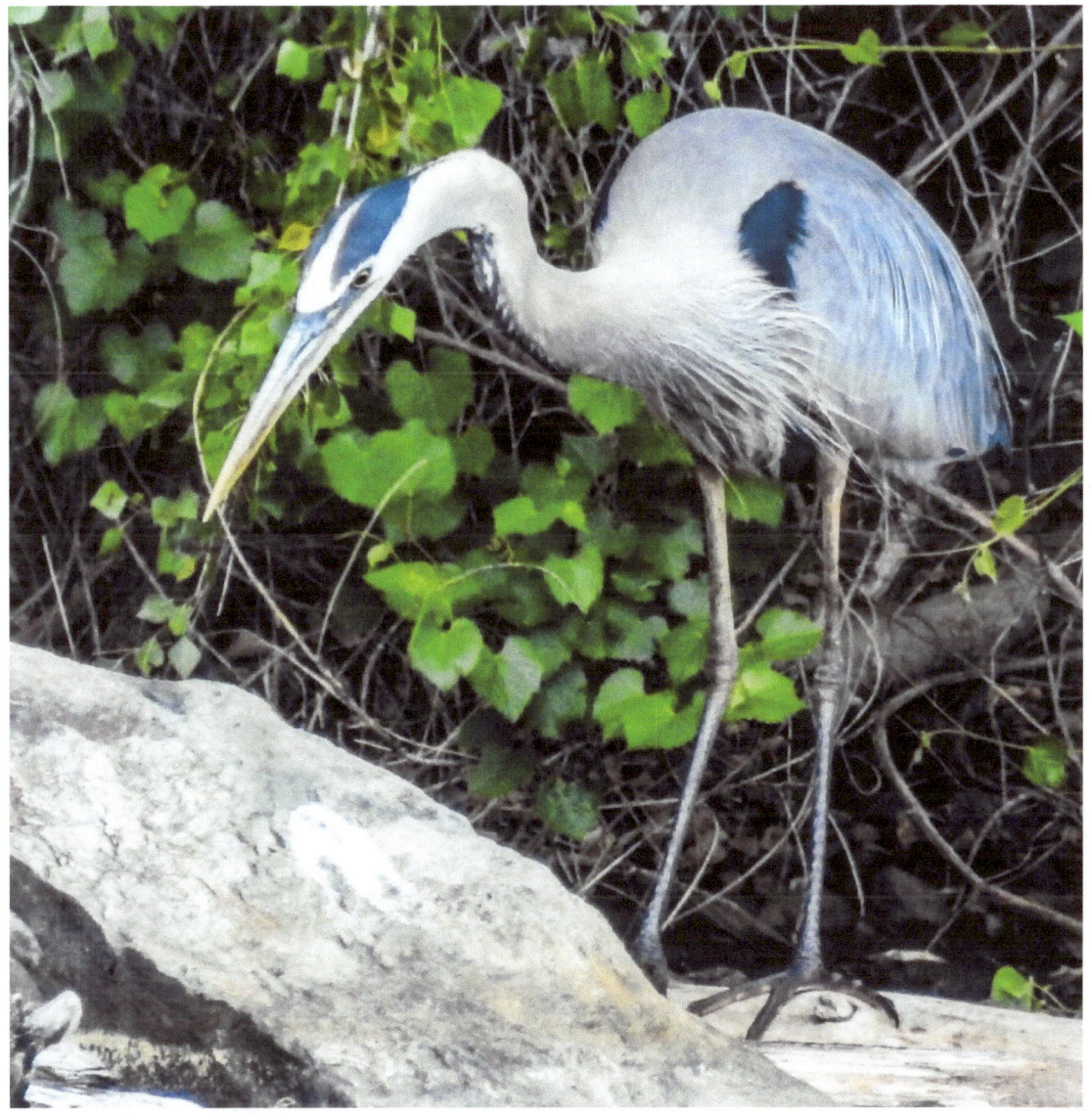

This picture illustrates many aspects of the mature, adult Great Blue Heron in non-breeding plumage. The dark blue patch on the top of the head is typical of a mature adult. By looking closely you can see that the dark plume starts at the center of the back of the head and trails down the neck. The darker blue patch on the shoulder also indicates maturity. Finally, the toes are toes are in their typical position when standing on a log.

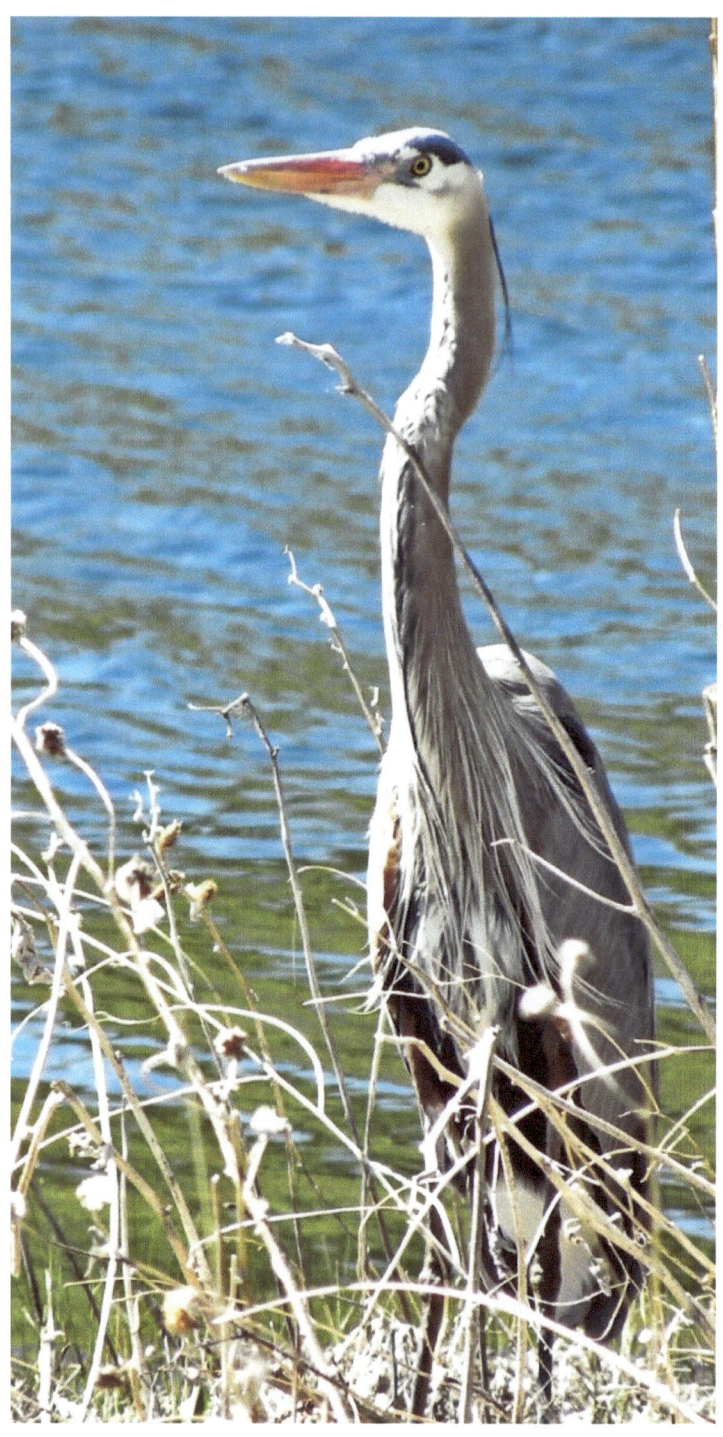

It is a little bit unusual to see a Great Blue Heron with its back toward the water. The dead plants indicate that it is winter. Some references do not show Arizona as a wintering area for Great Blue Herons, but they are in the central Arizona highlands throughout the year.

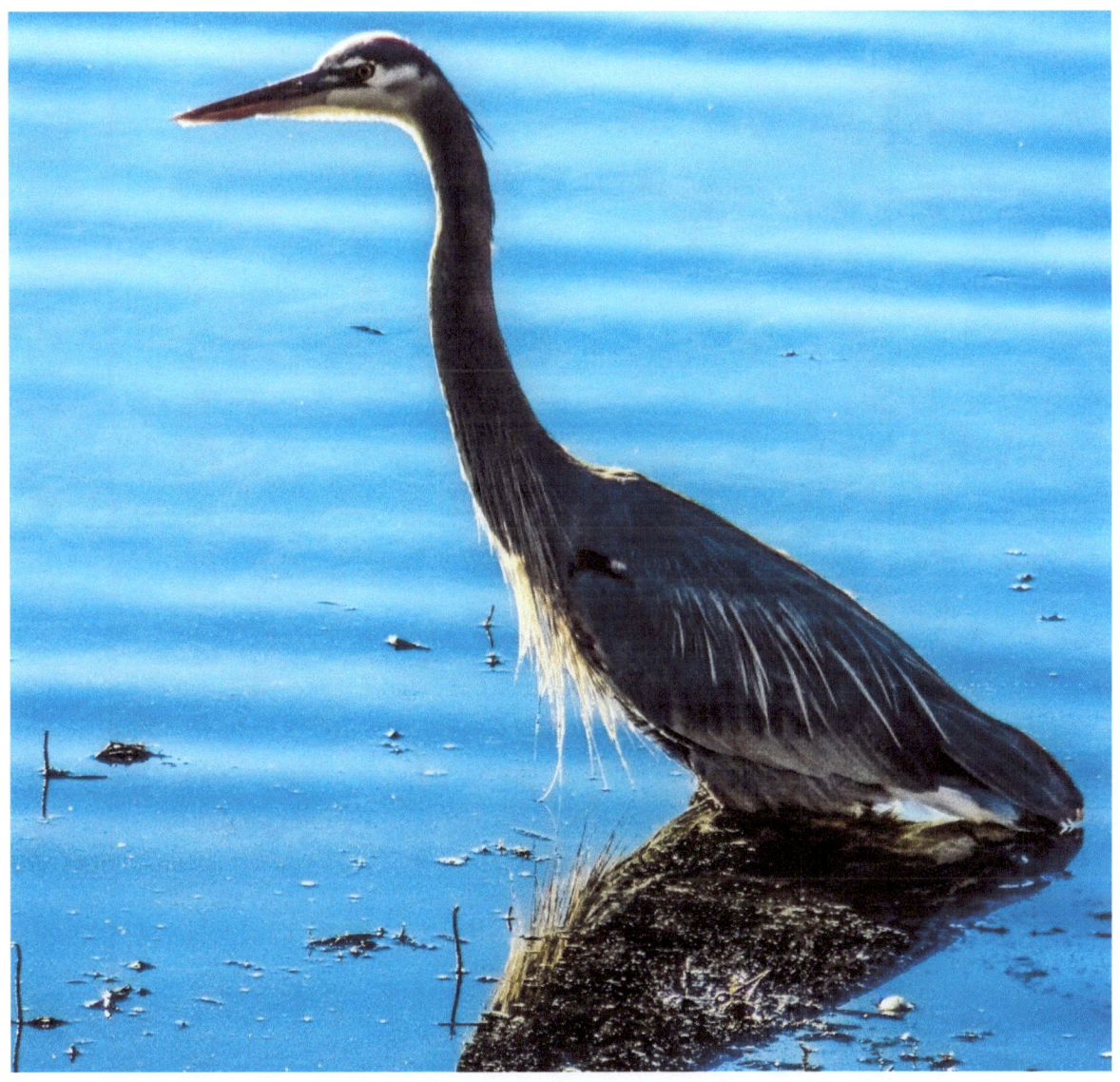

Standing in water up to its hips is another uncommon posture for a Great Blue Heron. Note the alertness of the bird as it stands motionless waiting for prey to approach. The shadow on the water produces an interesting play of light – making things more visible in the contrasting area.

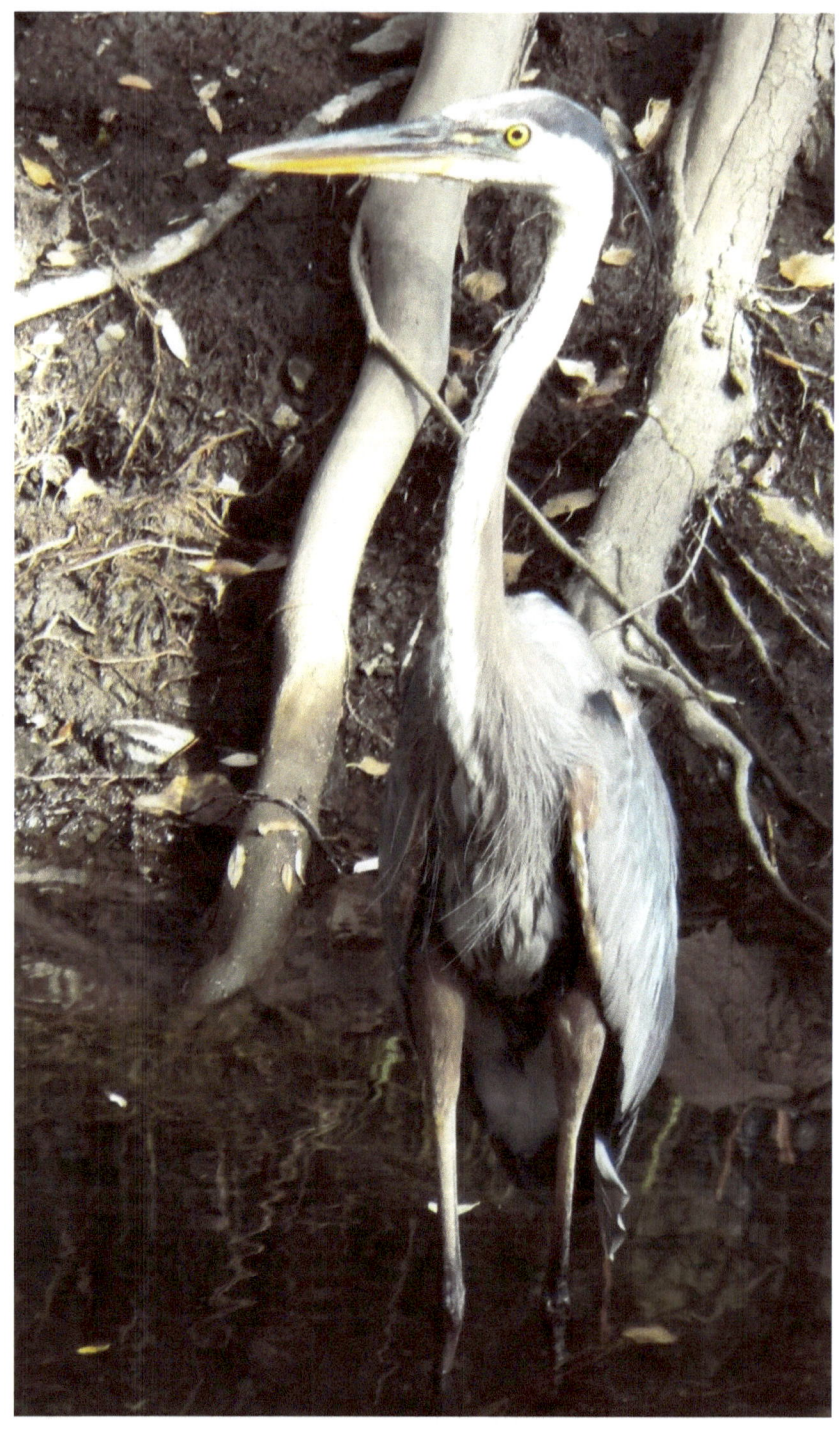

This bird is in a more typical pose – up to its knees in water. The trees on the bank in the background offer excellent camouflage for a Great Blue Heron. On the front portion of its left wing, the area lacking feathers is its wing patch. This will be more obvious when looking at pictures of the birds in flight.

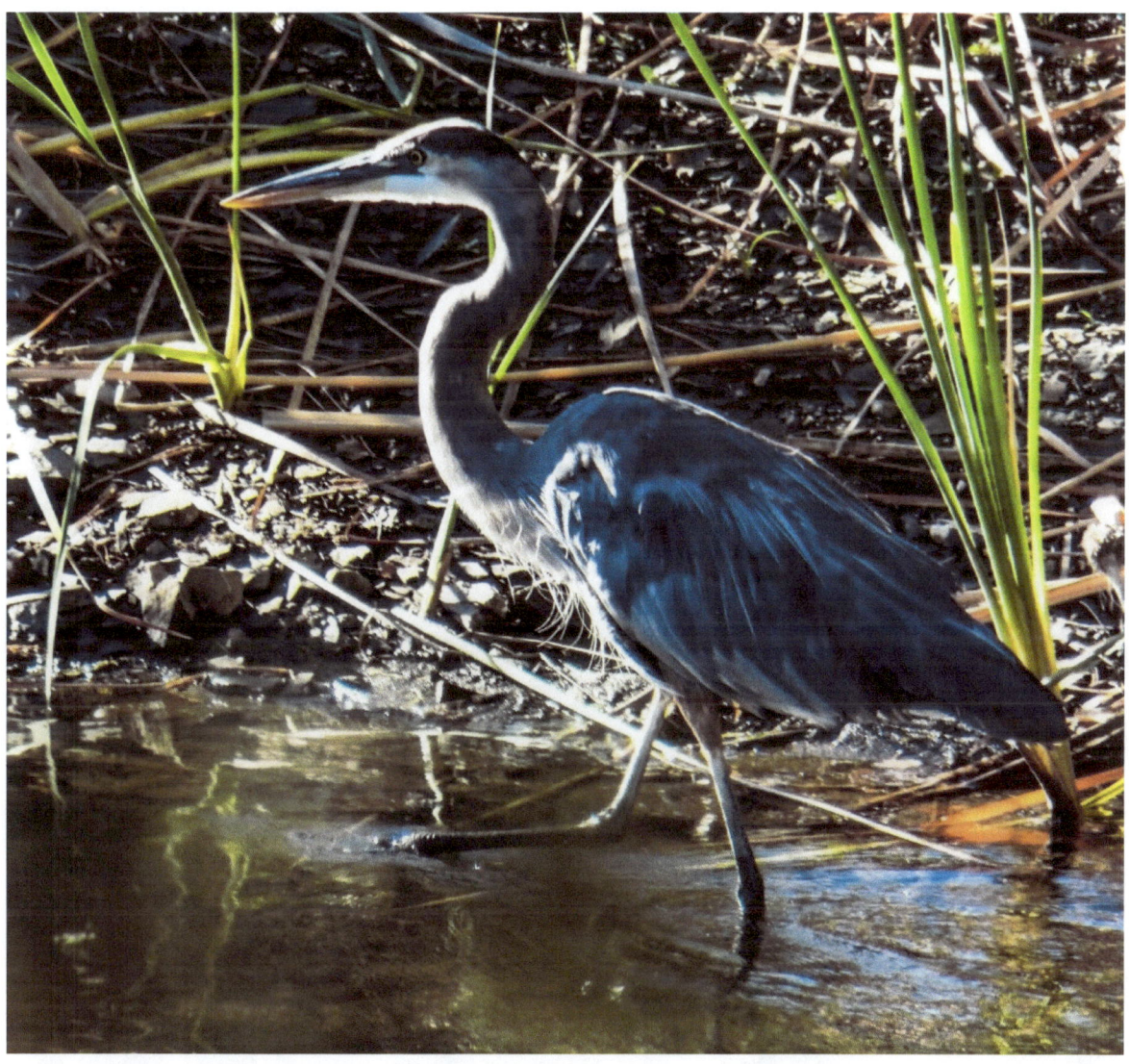

This Great Blue Heron is exhibiting a typical wading posture. The knee bends forward and then the ankle bends downward just at the water line. If a potential prey moved in response to the bird's motions, the bird is fully capable of striking from this position.

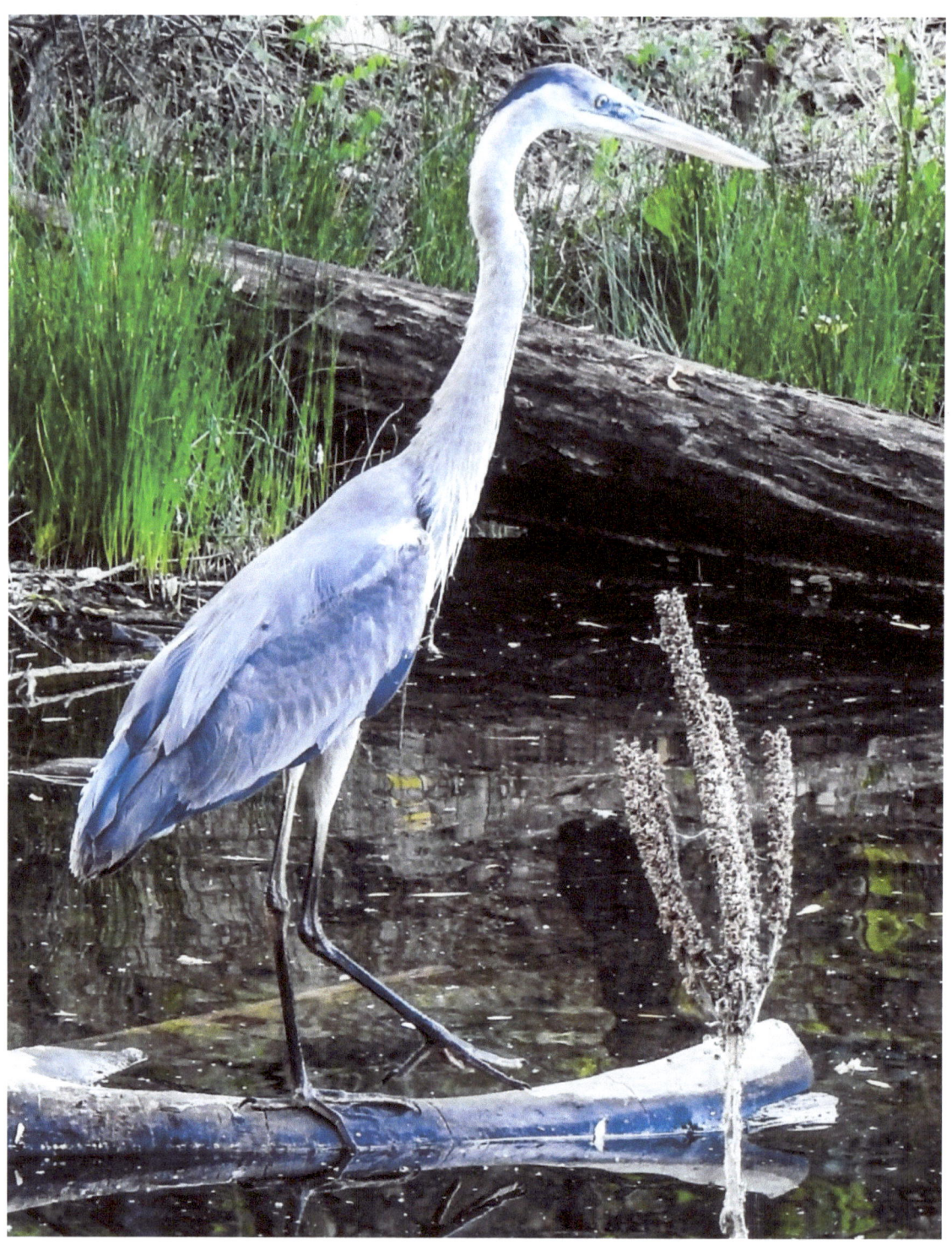

This pictures how a Great Blue Heron walks on a log. It moves very cautiously and remains alert for prey. The dried plant in the lower right is a mullein. It is an introduced species having been brought to North America by early colonists.

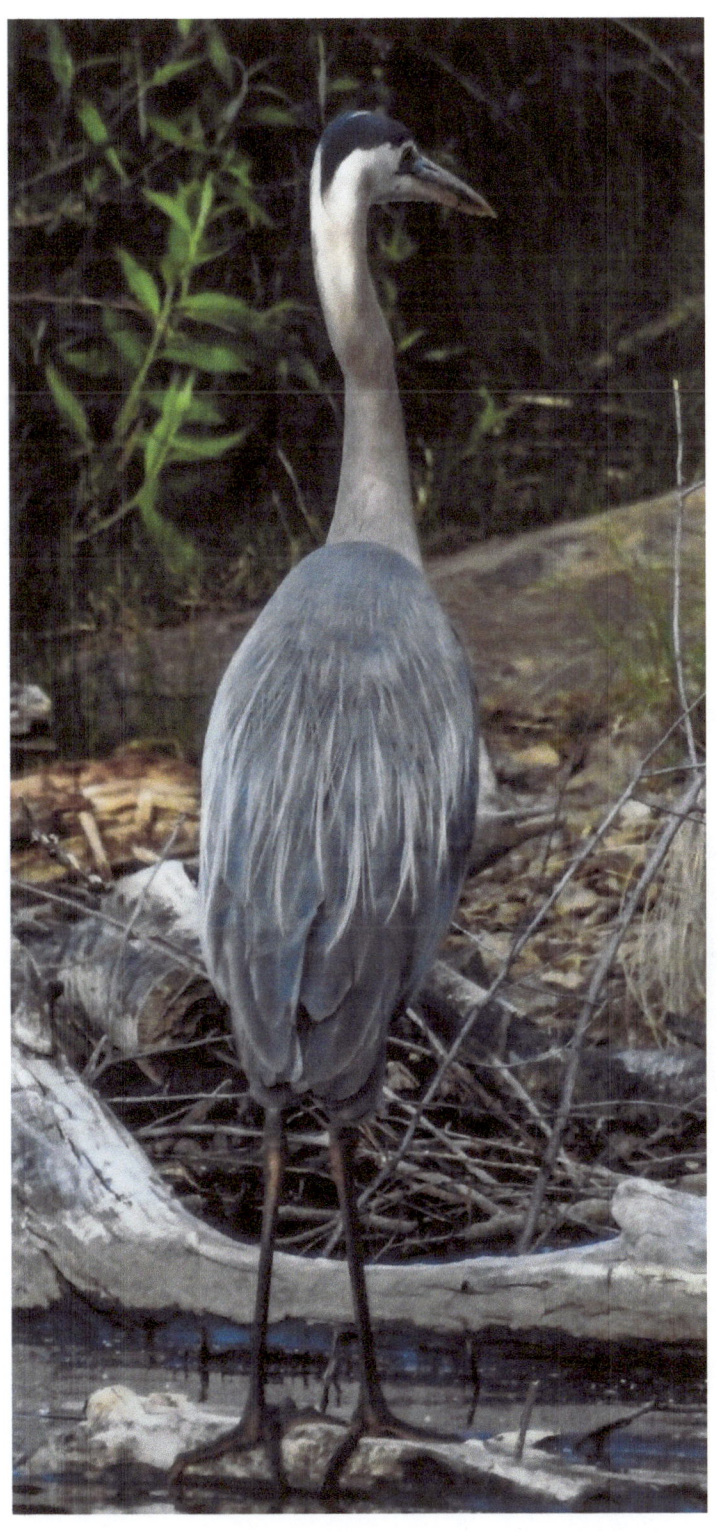

A full-body back view of a mature Great Blue Heron in non-breeding plumage.

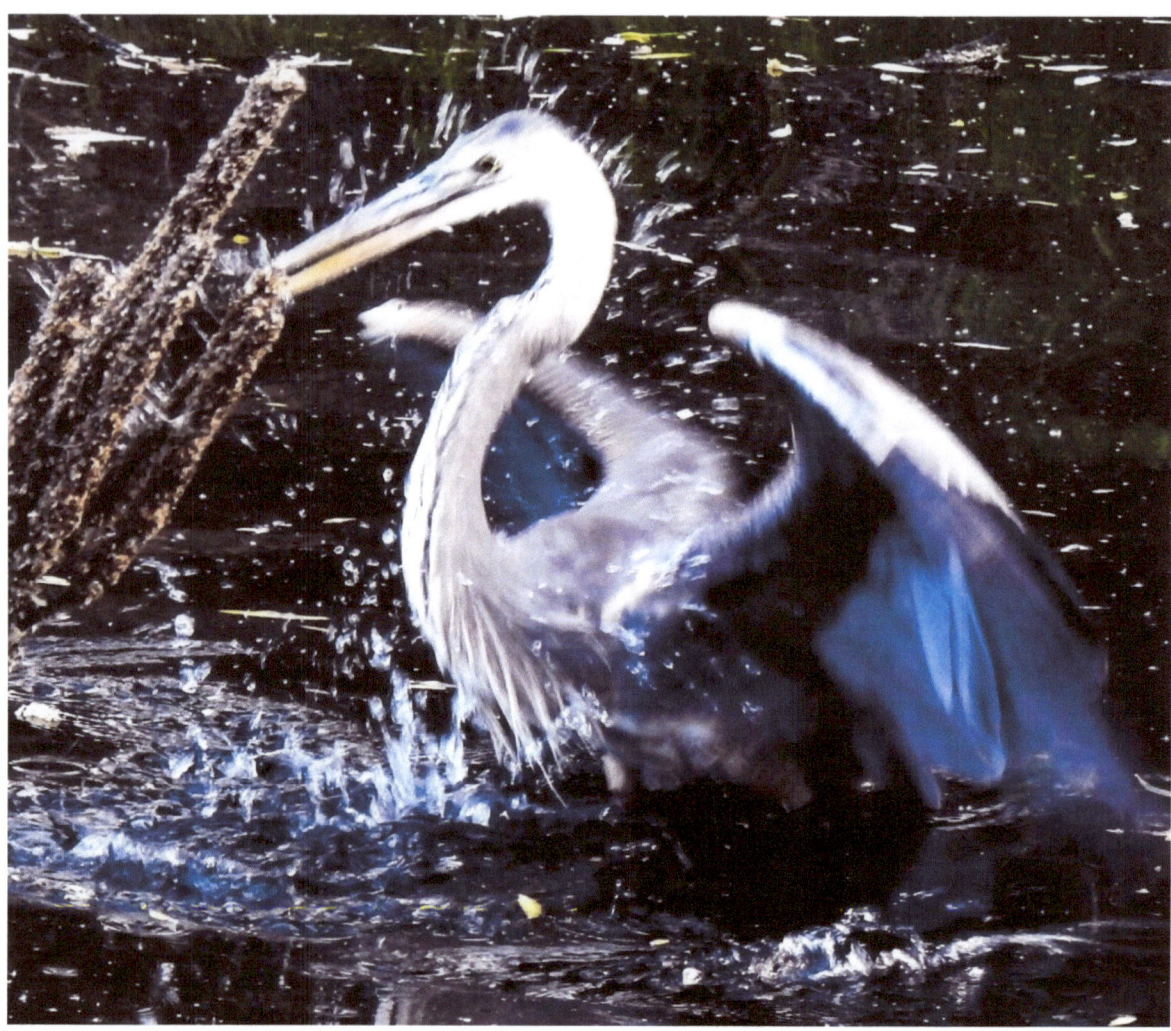

　　Although this Great Blue Heron came up with no catch, the wildlife artist has an advantage here over a photographer – a fish could be easily placed in this bird's bill. Do not follow the colors too closely in this rendition as they have been altered somewhat so that the water droplets being shaken off are more visible.

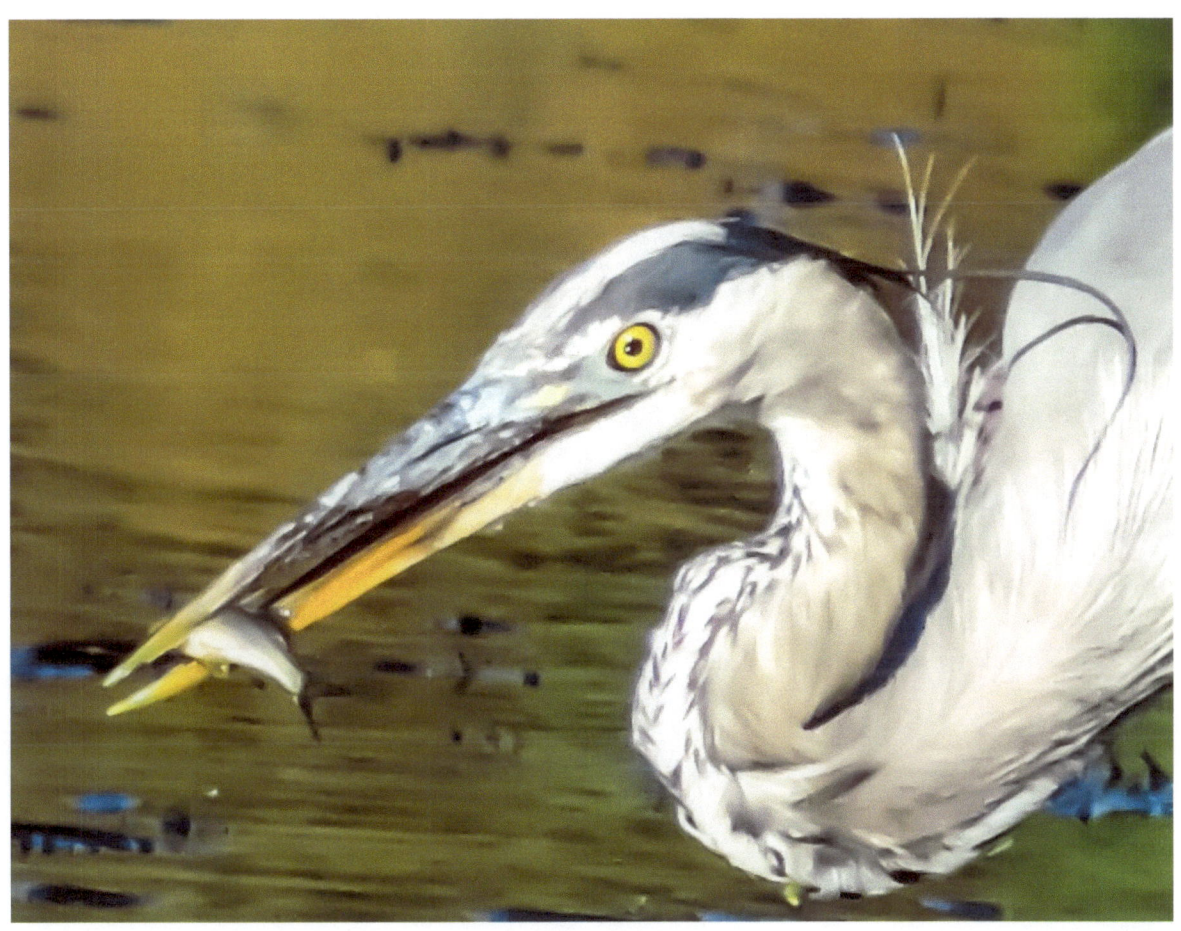

Success! Finally after about a half-hour of stalking this Great Blue Heron caught a fish. After crushing the fish in its strong bill, the bird will flip the fish up in the air and catch it head-first, swallowing it whole. The fish is always swallowed head first because the scales make it hard to swallow a fish tail first.

FLIGHT

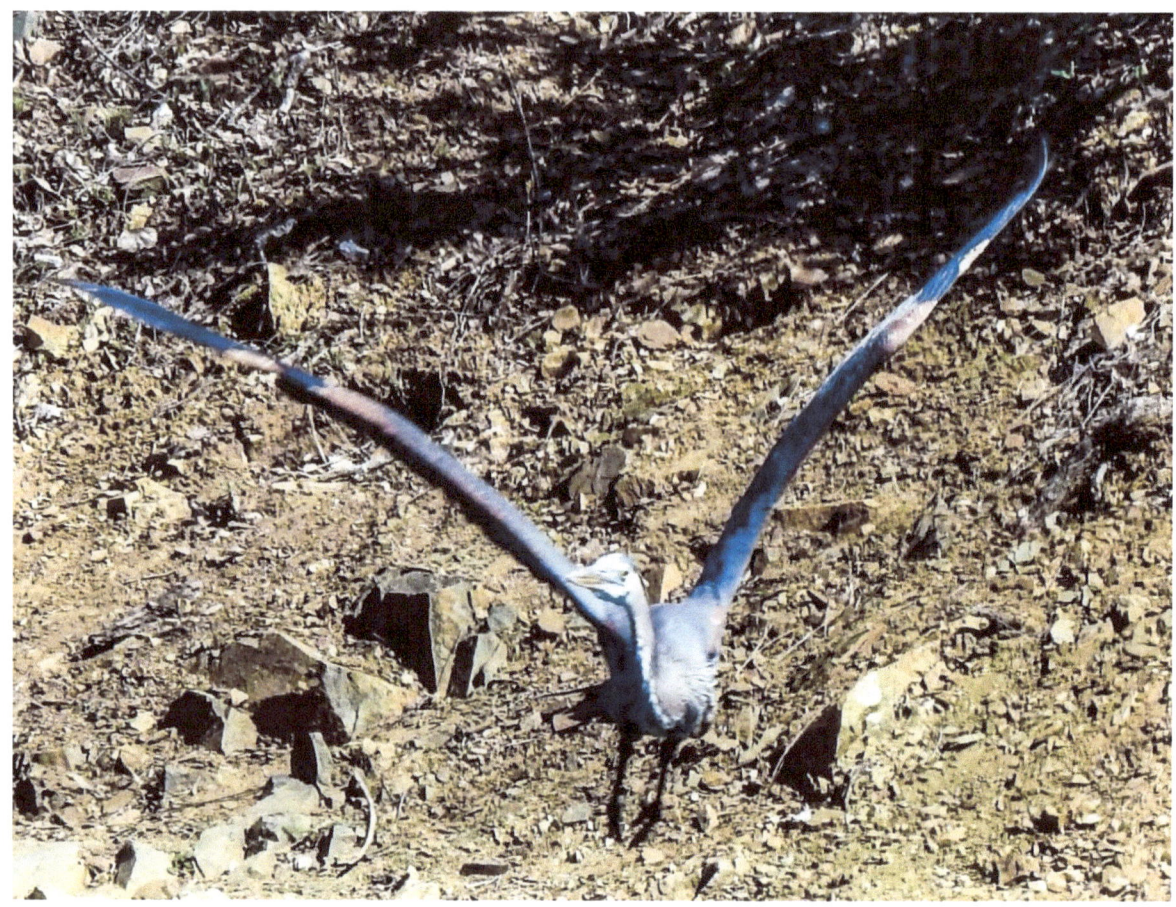

Note the wing patches in this picture. These appeared in earlier photographs as featherless areas on the wings particularly when the birds were perched. Great Blue Herons stand about 4 feet tall and have a wingspan of 6 feet.

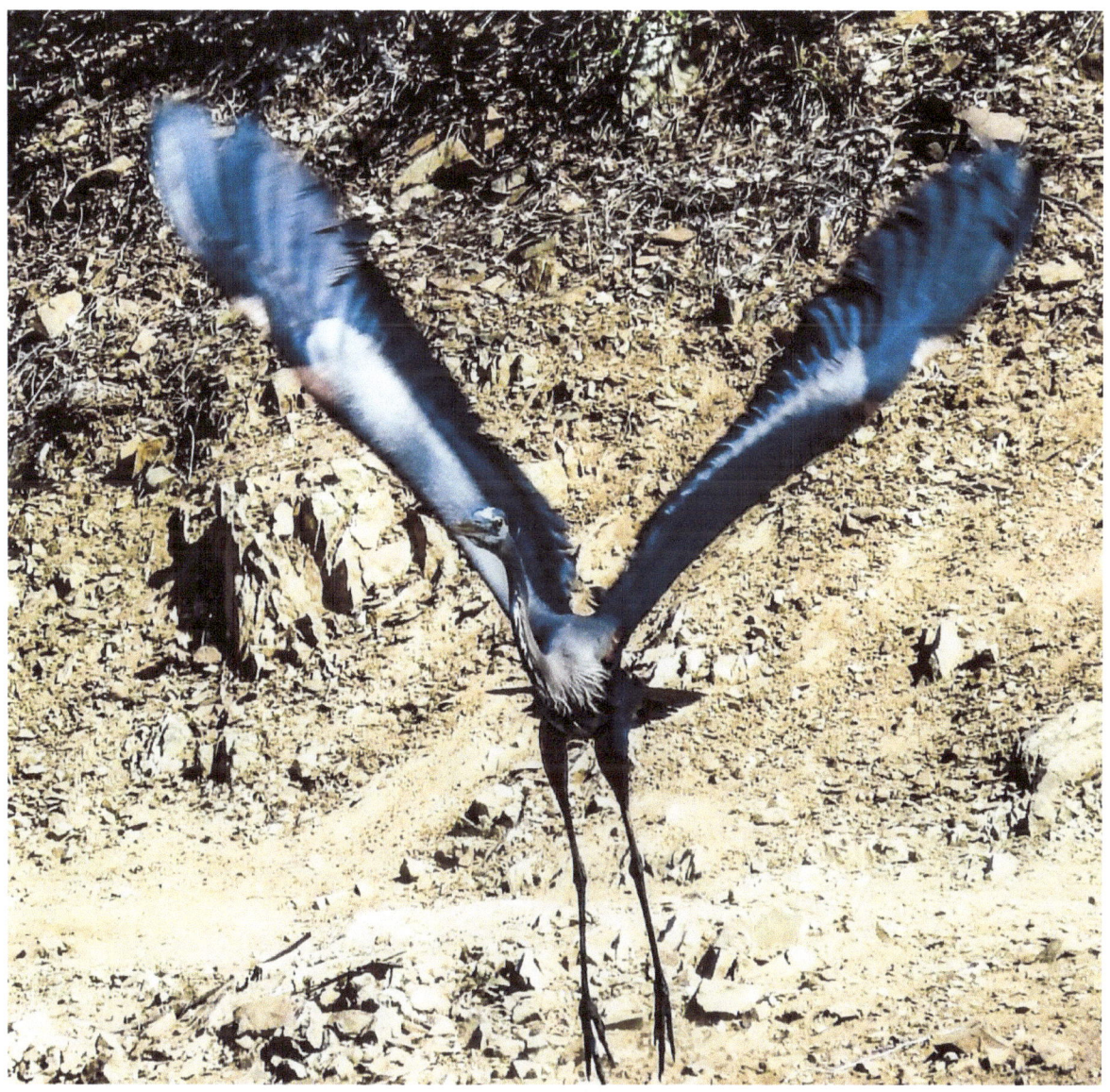

This picture illustrates how a Great Blue Heron takes off by jumping into the air.

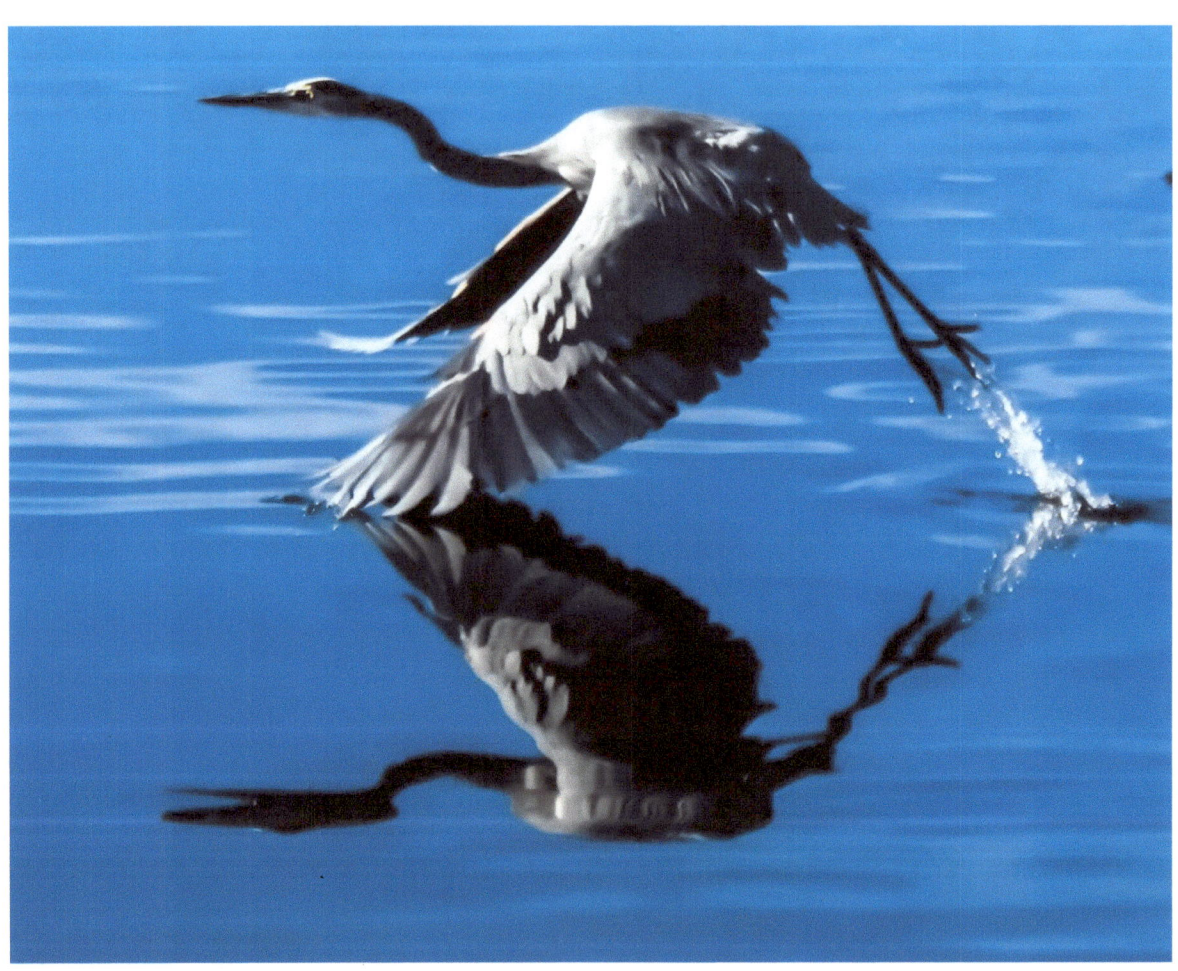

When taking off from a wading position, a Great Blue Heron jumps straight up out of the water. Note that the wings are actually dipping into the water for the first beat or two.

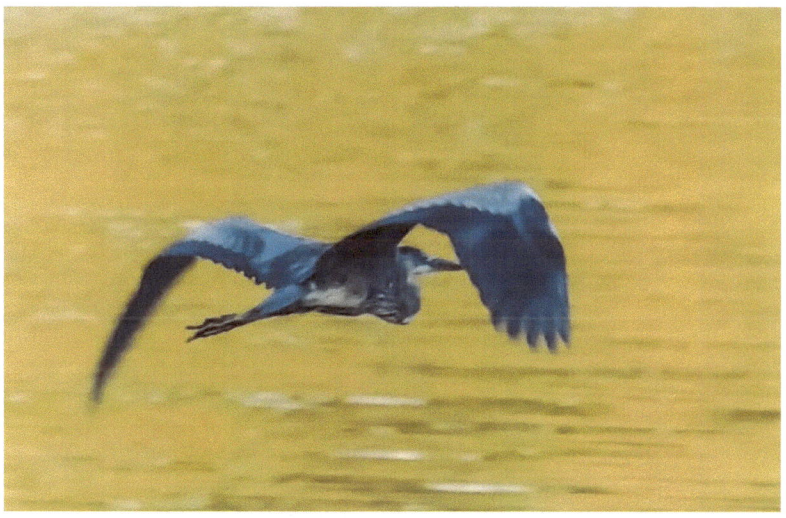

As a Great Blue Heron flattens out into level flight it tucks its head back and holds its feet straight behind the body. Herons are distinguished from cranes in flight by the position of the head – cranes fly with the head extended to the full length of the neck.

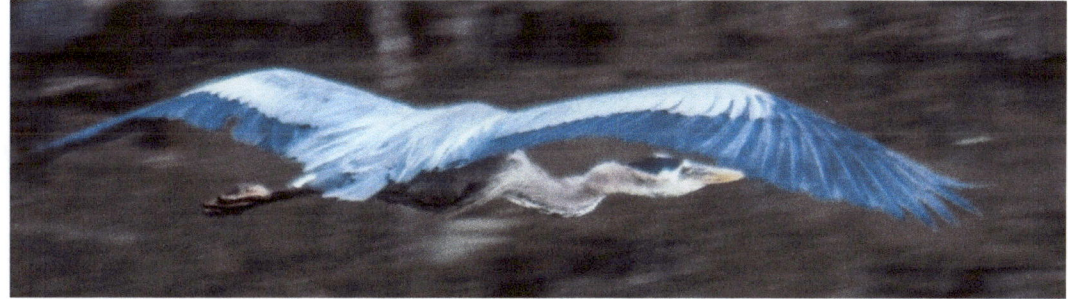

When a Great Blue Heron is about to land, it will extend its head but not usually to the full length of the neck.

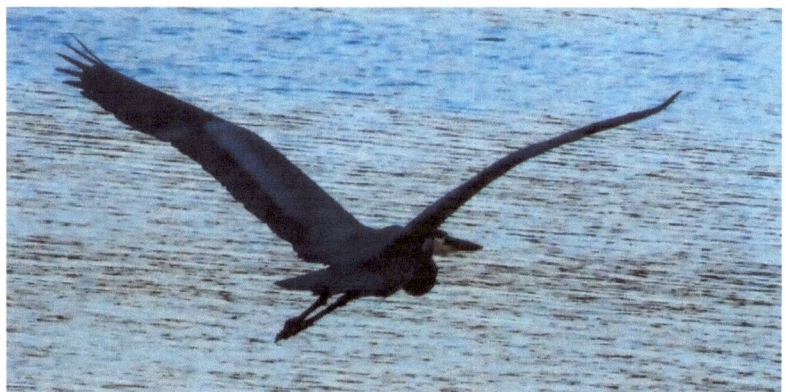

Slow, steady wing beats characterize a Great Blue Heron in flight.

CLOSE-UPS OF DETAILS

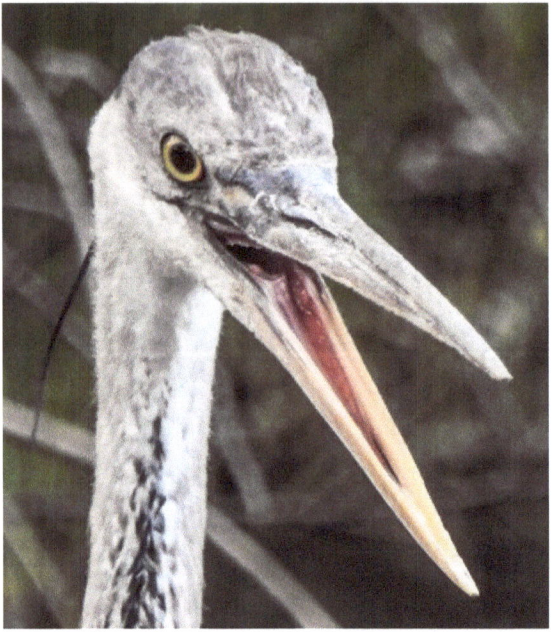

This bird is an immature as evidenced by its more solid gray head. However it is transitioning into adult plumage because it has a plume on the back of its head.

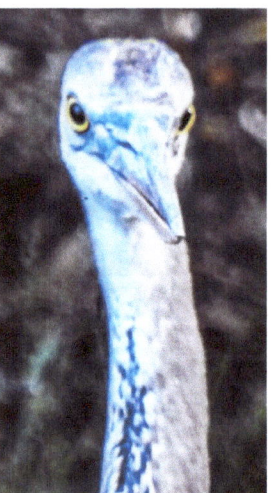

In this picture you can see that although a Great Blue Heron has eyes well on the side of its head they are able to move into a position giving it three dimensional vision. The color in this picture has been altered to emphasize the eyes.

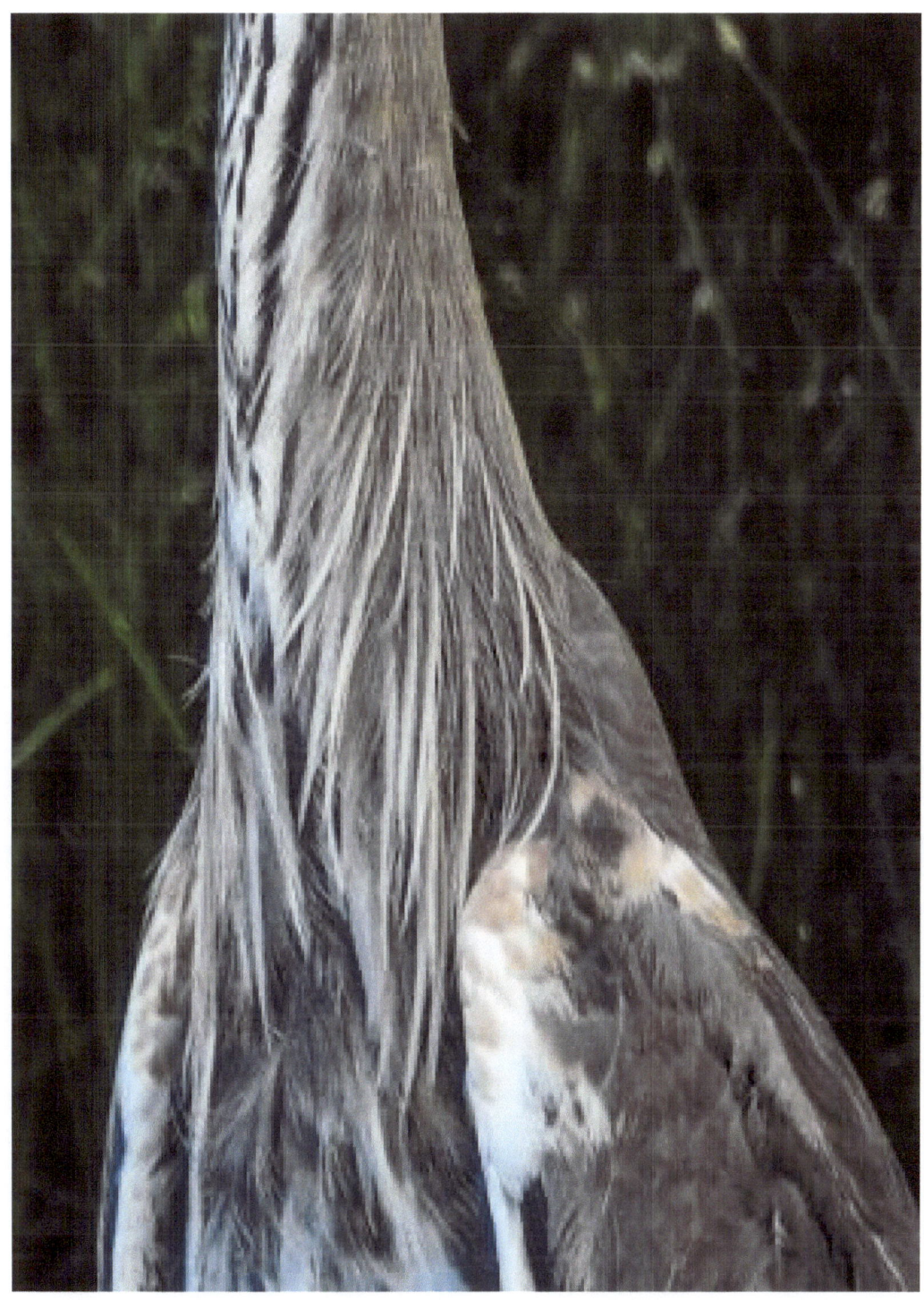

This picture illustrates the plumes that hang from the side of the neck and the tan wing patches at the shoulders of a Great Blue Heron. In a more mature bird the wing patches would be a little more reddish and slightly more extensive.

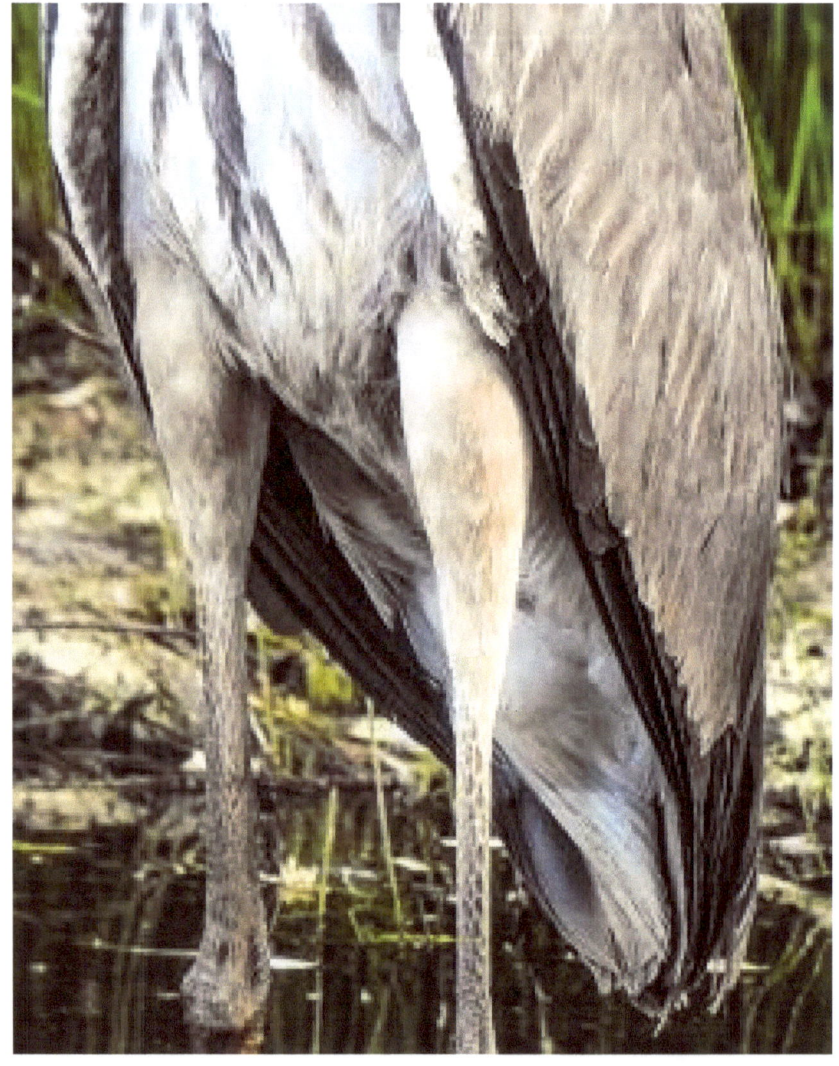

Of particular interest in this picture are the pattern of the scales on the legs of the Great Blue Heron.

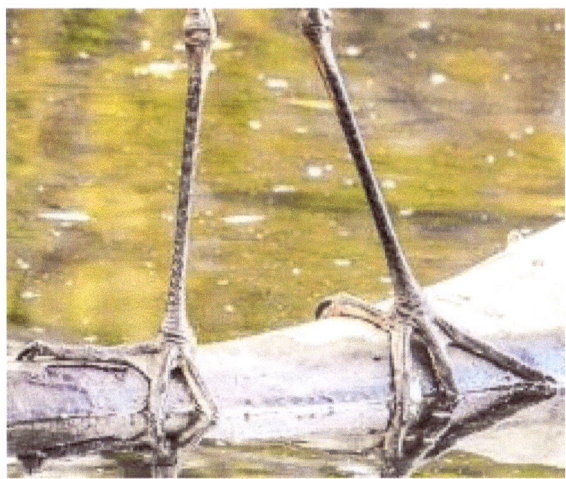

The very long toes of the Great Blue Heron are well adapted for grasping slippery logs in the wet habitat.

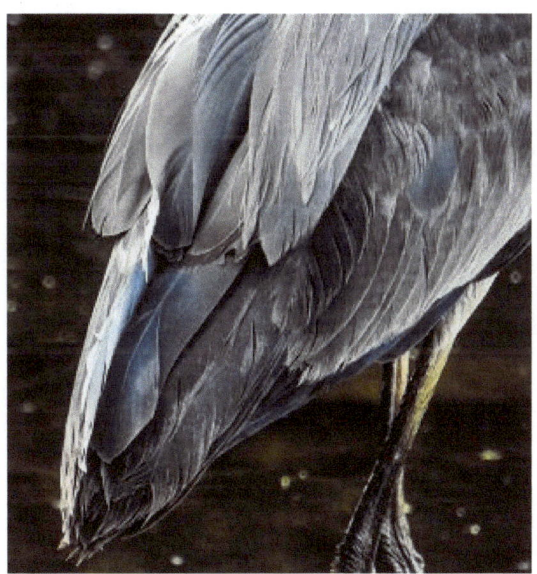

A fitting ending for the book is this illustration of how the wing and tail feathers overlap on a Great Blue Heron.

www.ingramcontent.com/pod-product-compliance
Lightning Source LLC
Chambersburg PA
CBHW050412180526
45159CB00005B/2248